PHOTOSYNTHESIS

PHOTOSYNTHESIS

Isaac Asimov

Basic Books, Inc., Publishers

New York   *London*

To the memory of henry blugerman

whose life was filled

with kindness and courage

Contents

Figures

PHOTOSYNTHESIS

I

The Great Cycle

The Ever-full

It's amazing how much we take for granted.

We breathe, for instance. We breathe constantly, sixteen times a minute. If we were to stop breathing for five minutes or so, we would die. Yet hardly anyone ever asks himself how it comes about that there is always something to breathe.

We breathe not merely to obtain air; we need a gas called "oxygen" which is found in the air. The air we draw into our lungs is about 21 per cent oxygen. Some of that oxygen is absorbed into our body and is used. The air we exhale is only 16 per cent oxygen.

Over and over, it is 21 per cent oxygen going in and only 16 per cent oxygen going out. Not only you and I do it, but every human being on earth, and every land animal as well. The animals of the sea and of fresh water don't breathe as we do, but they extract and consume the oxygen dissolved in the water. Plants consume oxygen, too, in certain of their life-processes. Bacteria in bringing about rot and decay also consume oxygen* and so do various natural chemical processes on Earth that do not involve life-forms.

Oxygen, then, is constantly being consumed, and you and I (along with other oxygen-consuming life forms) replace it by another gas known as "carbon dioxide." The exchange is a poor one in a way for we cannot breathe it in place of oxygen. The concentration of carbon dioxide in air is so low at this time that it cannot hurt us in any way, but if that concentration builds up moderately, it would suffocate us.

* Some types of bacteria do not consume oxygen, but they represent a tiny minority of all life.

3

As a result of all the breathing and other oxygen-consuming processes that take place on Earth, it would seem that some 10,000 tons of oxygen are used up every second. At that rate the last scrap of usable oxygen in the earth's atmosphere and ocean would be gone in 3,000 years.

Nor would we have to wait a full 3,000 years to be in serious trouble. After a few centuries, the amount of carbon dioxide that would have accumulated in the atmosphere would suffocate all animal life.

Yet mankind, and all of life, has been consuming oxygen and producing carbon dioxide not for a few hundred years only, or for a few thousand years, but for hundreds of millions of years at least. And despite the fact that oxygen has been constantly disappearing for all that time, the air remains a cornucopia—an ever-full horn of plenty. There is still just as much oxygen in the air as there ever was; and just as little carbon dioxide.

Why?

The only reasonable conjecture is that some "cycle" exists. Affairs move in a circle and everything returns, so to speak, as quickly as it leaves.

We can see such a cycle with respect to fresh water. We are always drinking fresh water and using it for washing and for industrial purposes. Millions of gallons are consumed each minute the world over, and for each gallon man consumes, many gallons run off the earth's land surfaces unused by man—yet the fresh water is never entirely consumed.

But that paradox has a plain answer. All the fresh water, used or unused, evaporates, either directly from its place or after it has run off into the ocean. The Sun's heat draws vast quantities of vapor upward from the ocean and land; and *only* water vapor, not any of the dissolved solids present there.

The vapor returns to earth as rainfall and the supply of fresh water is replenished as quickly as it is consumed.

Presumably, then, there is some process on the earth that forms oxygen as quickly as we, and other forms of life, consume it. There must also be some process that consumes carbon dioxide as quickly as we produce it. Only in that case could we expect the oxygen and carbon dioxide level of the atmosphere to remain steady over millions upon millions of years.

The process that restores the oxygen and removes the carbon dioxide, and keeps the atmosphere breathable, is, however, nowhere near as obvious as the process that restores the fresh water and keeps the land pleasantly moist and the lakes and rivers sparklingly full.

To find the process, let us consider another, and rather similar problem; one that may be related to the problem of oxygen and carbon dioxide levels.

It is this: Why don't we run out of food?

When we breathe oxygen, it combines with some of the substances in our tissues to produce the energy we need to live. In the process, we form not only carbon dioxide, which we breathe out, but also an assortment of other waste products that are eliminated chiefly by way of the urine.

If we do nothing but breathe, then eventually, so much of the substance of our tissues is combined with oxygen in order to produce energy that not enough is left to keep us alive. We lose weight, grow gaunt and feeble, and, eventually, die.

To prevent this, we must build up our tissues as fast as they are consumed, and for that purpose we must eat. We must take into our own body the components of the tissues of other animals, for instance, and convert them into tissue of our own.

But the animals we eat have been using up their tissues for their own purposes and have themselves had to replace what they consume by eating. If every animal were to try to replenish its consumed tissues by eating other animals, then all animal life would quickly come to an end, because all the tissue substance would come to an end. The stronger, larger animals would rob the substance of the smaller animals, then fall each upon the other. And, finally, one animal would be left and it would slowly starve to death.

If animals are to stay alive, then, they must find some source of food which doesn't have to eat, but which can produce its tissue substances "out of nothing."

This would seem an impossibility (if we didn't know the answer in advance) but it isn't. The answer is plant life. All animals eat plants, or other animals that have eaten plants, or other animals that have eaten animals that have eaten plants, and so on. In the end, it all comes back to plants.

Plants are made up of tissues containing the same complex substances animal tissues do. Animals can live, then, by feeding on plants exclusively, robbing them of their tissue stores and putting them to the use of the eater. Most animals are indeed "herbivorous," that is plant-eating. A minority are "carnivorous" (meat eating) and prey on the herbivorous majority. A few types of creatures, such as men, pigs and rats, are "omnivorous" (all-eating) and can make use of plants or animals—or almost anything, for that matter—with equal ease. Omnivorous creatures are generally quite successful in the scheme of life.

Plants themselves make use of their own tissue substance to obtain energy. Yet despite their own use and of the depredations made upon them by animal life, the plants of the world are never entirely consumed. Their tissues are replaced as quickly as they are used up and they do not have to raid the supply of other organisms to replace it. They do indeed seem to form tissue "out of nothing."

Thanks to this ability on the part of the plants, the food supply of the world, like the oxygen supply, remains eternally full.

Plants somehow supply the food. It must, somehow, come from somewhere. It can't really form "out of nothing." Let us tackle the plant, then, and if we find out something about how the food supply is restored, we may also find out something about how the oxygen supply of the air is restored.

The Willow Tree

Of course, it is quite obvious that plants don't manufacture their substance out of nothing in any literal sense. There are well-known facts that make that quite impossible.

A plant begins as a tiny seed, but that seed wouldn't grow and develop into a large plant (sometimes even a huge one) unless it were placed in soil.

Once in the soil, the growing plant developed a complex root system that forced its way through the soil in every direction. If the plant were pulled out of the soil, or if its roots were badly damaged in some way, it would die.

It seemed clear that plants obtained some kind of nourishment from the soil through its roots. That nourishment was nothing that animals could eat, but clearly it was something that plants could thrive on.

Not all soil was equally suitable for plants. There was fertile soil in which plants could grow readily, and barren soil in which they could grow only poorly if at all. Some sort of nourishing material was present in the fertile soil that was absent in the barren soil.

What's more, if fertile soil were used to grow crop after crop of a particular sort of plant, that soil gradually lost its fertility, as though the supply of nourishment in it were used up. Some of this fertility could be restored if the land were allowed to remain uncultivated for a period of time, or if a change of crop were grown on it. Even better, the land might be made more fertile by adding to it certain substances such as animal wastes ("fertilizers").

The soil was not the only thing required for healthy plant life, however. Another factor, just as vital, was water. Any farmer knew that no soil, however rich and fertile, could possibly yield a crop without an ample supply of water. A period of drought was deadly to those farmers who depended on a more or less steady rainfall. Those farmers who lived near rivers worked up extensive systems of canals to bring river water to fields, especially in regions where rain was scanty.

Indeed, the first human civilizations were built up in irrigated river valleys—the Nile in Egypt, the Euphrates in Mesopotamia, the Indus in Pakistan, and the Yellow in China.

One might easily assume that of the two, soil and water, it was the soil, really, that was the more important. The solid plant is much more like the solid soil than it is like the liquid water. It is easier to suppose that the solid material of the soil is somehow changed into the solid materials of plant tissue, than that water would set and harden and become alive.

The purpose of the water, one could suppose, was merely to transport material from the soil into the plant's interior. Naturally, if water were not present, materials from the soil could not be carried into the plant and growth would halt. Water would be necessary to plant life—but only in a passive way.

It wasn't until the beginning of modern times that anyone thought of checking this by experiment.

The man who had the thought was Jan Baptista van Helmont, an alchemist and physician of the Low Countries, who lived and worked in territory that is now Belgium, but was then part of the Spanish monarchy.

Van Helmont had the notion that water was the fundamental substance of the universe (as, in fact, certain ancient Greek philosophers had maintained). If so, everything was really water, and substances that didn't look like water were nevertheless water that had merely changed its form in some fashion.

For instance, water was necessary to plant life. Could it be, then, that, unlikely as it might seem on the surface, plant tissue was formed out of water, rather than out of soil? Why not try and see?

In 1648, Van Helmont concluded his great experiment, great

not only because it produced interesting and even crucial results, but because it was the first quantitative experiment ever conducted that involved a living organism. It was the first biological experiment, in other words, in which substances were weighed accurately and the carefully noted changes in weights supplied the answer being sought.

Van Helmont had begun by transplanting the shoot of a young willow tree into a large bucket of soil. He weighed the willow tree and the soil separately. Now if the willow tree formed its tissues by absorbing substances from the soil, then, as the willow tree gained weight, the soil would lose weight. Van Helmont carefully kept the soil covered so that no materials could fall into the bucket and confuse the manner in which the soil lost that weight.

Naturally, Van Helmont had to water the willow tree; it wouldn't grow otherwise. If, however, water were only a transport medium, it would merely act to carry material from soil to plant and then evaporate. The water he had to keep adding would then serve only to replace that lost by evaporation.

For five years, Van Helmont watered his tree with rainwater. It grew and flourished and at the end of the time, he carefully removed it from the bucket, knocked the soil from its roots and weighed it. In five years of growing, the willow tree had added 164 pounds to its weight.

Very good! Now to weigh the soil after it had been dried. Had it lost 164 pounds to the tree? Not at all. It had lost only two ounces!

The willow tree had gained a great deal of weight—but not from the soil. What was the only other substance that made contact with the willow tree, Van Helmont asked himself. The answer was: Water.

From this, he deduced that it was from water that the plant drew its substance, *not* from the soil. He used the results of this experiment to argue that water was indeed the fundamental substance of the universe, since if it could change to plant tissue it could surely change to anything else as well.

Air

But let's see what Van Helmont really did prove.

He did indeed show that the soil was not the main source of plant tissue. At least, he showed it for the willow tree—but we can safely assume, as scientists have long since amply demonstrated, that it is so for all other plants as well.

The root system that works its way snakily through large stretches of soil cannot be considered as acting to absorb soil primarily, with or without water transport.

But then did Van Helmont prove that the soil was no source *at all* for plant tissue? No, he didn't. There was some loss in the weight of the soil—two ounces. That isn't much, and it may even be the result of what we call "experimental error" for it is hard to weigh *all* the soil; some must have clung to the roots; and the balances of the day were not as accurate as those we have now. Still, a two ounce loss is something. Could it represent the abstraction from the soil of certain minor, but necessary, components of plant tissue.

Then, too, Van Helmont's observations, however accurate, did not make earlier observations false. If a theory is to be useful, it must explain *all* observations. For instance, it remains a fact, despite Van Helmont's willow tree, that some soil is fertile and some barren; that soil loses fertility with overuse and can regain it with the addition of fertilizer.

Soil, then, must contribute something. If not all, at least something, and that something must be vital. For instance, if soil is not a major source of nourishment, then it ought to be possible to grow plants in water, without the presence of soil. This is clearly so in the case of water plants such as seaweed, but it ought to be true of land plants also, if the willow tree is a guide.

If Van Helmont's conclusion is accurate and water is the *only* source of plant nourishment, then plants should, in fact, grow in completely pure water ("distilled water"). They do not; they grow only briefly in distilled water.

But what if certain minor soil components are necessary? These components, once identified, can be added to the distilled water in small quantities and growth might then take place without soil. This does indeed turn out to be practical, and the cultivation of plants in solutions rather than in soil is known as "hydroponics" or "tank farming."

Let us allow, then, that certain minor soil constituents are necessary for plant growth and are incorporated into plant tissue. That still leaves the great bulk of plant tissue to be accounted for. If we accept Van Helmont's contention that water was indeed the only material, other than the soil itself, that touched the plant, then we must accept his conclusion that the plant tissue was derived from water. But is his contention really so?

Surely water was not the only material that touched the plant. Air touched it as well.

Van Helmont could scarcely have failed to realize that air touched the plant. Yet he dismissed the matter.

Air, in general, was dismissed by philosophers prior to Van Helmont's time. They knew it existed, of course, since one can scarcely argue with a windstorm. Nevertheless, air couldn't be seen or touched. It seemed to be a tenuous nothing that might blow about but did not interact with the liquids and solids one could see and touch. Air tended to be ignored, therefore, by alchemists and others who dealt with the physical materials of the universe.

The alchemists of ancient and medieval times occasionally noticed that vapors formed in their mixtures and came bubbling off. All such vapors were thought to be forms of air, however, and they, too, were dismissed.

In fact the very first person we know of to pay attention to such vapors and to decide that they were more than merely forms of air was Van Helmont himself. He noted that some of the vapors he formed in the course of his experiments simply didn't act like air. Some vapors could be made to burst into flame, for instance, and air itself never did so. Why then, given Van Helmont's special interest in vapors, did he ignore the possibility of air as a source of plant nourishment?

Van Helmont noticed that when inflammable vapors burned, they sometimes left behind droplets of moisture. These vapors, therefore, seemed to him to be still other forms of water. Ordinary air apparently had nothing to do with water and therefore, by Van Helmont's pet theory, air could not be a form of matter. It was on that basis that he ignored it as a possible source of plant nourishment.

To Van Helmont, those vapors that seemed to be a form of water nevertheless differed from ordinary water in an important way. Like air, they couldn't be seen or felt, and didn't have a definite volume. Instead, the vapors were a form of matter which spread every which way through any volume they could penetrate.

The ancient Greeks had imagined that the universe began with matter in just a higgledy-piggledy unorganized form. They called matter in this form "chaos." Van Helmont (some people think) applied this term to vapor, pronouncing it in Lowland fashion. If the word is spelled as it was then pronounced, it becomes "gas."

The word eventually caught on, and was used not only for vapors, but for air as well; and, indeed, for all substances that shared the chief properties of air.

Oddly enough, Van Helmont was the first to take note of a gas that was to prove an important key to the problem of plant nutrition (had he but known!). When he burned wood, he obtained a gas which he called "gas sylvestre" ("gas from wood"). The gas itself was not inflammable but it tended to dissolve in water (or "turn into water" as Van Helmont would suppose). That gas is the one we now know as carbon dioxide.

One of the difficulties of studying gases lies in the very fact that they are chaotic. Once they are produced, they bubble away, spread out, mix with the air and are lost.

An important step, in this respect, was taken by Stephen Hales, an English botanist who lived a century after Van Helmont. He studied, in considerable detail, the manner in which water passed through the plant, being absorbed at the roots and being given off again, as vapor, at the leaves. The ability of the plants to give off a gas made it seem to him that it was possible that plants could take up gases also; that they could, in effect, breathe as animals do, though less obviously. And if so, he thought, it was possible that air might serve as a source of nourishment for at least part of plant tissue.

This impelled him to study gases and, in 1727, to publish the results of these studies. From his publication we see that he prepared his gases in such a way as not to allow them to escape. The reaction vessel in which they were formed was closed, except for a curved tube leading out and under the surface of the water in an open trough. Under water the tube turned up and opened into the mouth of a water-filled jar, up-ended in the trough.

The gas bubbling into the up-ended jar rose to the top and forced the water out through the bottom. When the water was all forced out, a glass slide could be pushed over the mouth of the jar and it could then be turned right-side up. It would be full of a particular gas, in relatively pure form. That gas could then be studied at leisure.

Hales prepared and studied, in this fashion, a number of gases, including those we now call hydrogen, sulfur dioxide, methane, carbon monoxide and carbon dioxide.

Hales didn't get as much out of it as he might have, for he was convinced that all these gases were merely modified forms of air. He didn't realize that he was dealing with different and distinct substances. Nevertheless, his method of preparing gases stimulated the intensive study of air and other gaseous substances during the remainder of the eighteenth century.

Oxygen

The intense and continuing interest in gases soon made it clear, once and for all, that many gases were distinct substances quite different from air. Indeed, chemists began to suspect that air itself might consist of more than one kind of gas.

A Scottish chemist, Joseph Black, was particularly interested in carbon dioxide (he called it "fixed air"). In 1756, he found it would combine with lime to form limestone. The interesting point, though, was that he did not have to add carbon dioxide to the lime. If he simply allowed the lime to stand in the open air, it slowly began to powder away at the edges and became limestone. Apparently small quantities of carbon dioxide were present in the air at all times, so that air contained at least one minor gaseous component. If one, might there not be more?

In 1772, another Scottish chemist, Daniel Rutherford (a student of Black's, as a matter of fact), reported on the effects of allowing candles to burn in a closed container of air. Eventually, the candle would no longer burn and the air that remained in the container would not support the burning of anything else either.

By this time it was known that burning candles produced carbon dioxide and that nothing would burn in carbon dioxide. That seemed the easiest explanation, then, for what had happened. The burning candle had used up all the air and replaced it with carbon dioxide.

But it was also known that certain chemicals would absorb carbon dioxide. The used-up air was passed through these chemicals and the carbon dioxide produced by the burning candle was absorbed. The air did not vanish, however, as it ought to have if it were nothing but carbon dioxide. Most of it remained. This remaining part of the air was not carbon dioxide and so Rutherford thought that now, with the latter removed, a candle would once more burn in the air that was left—yet it did not.

In other words, Rutherford had a gas that was a major part of the air, but was not all of it; that was not carbon dioxide and yet would not support the burning of a candle. He reported all this but was unable to interpret it correctly.

Just two years later, an English Unitarian minister and amateur chemist, Joseph Priestley, added another important item to growing knowledge about gases.

He had grown interested in gases through the accident that his church in Leeds was next door to a brewery. In the process of beer production, a gas is produced (the one responsible for bubbles in beer) and Priestley could obtain quantities of this gas. He collected other gases, too, as Hales had done, but led them through mercury rather than water. Thus, he could isolate and study those gases which were soluble in water and would not survive in gaseous form if they were bubbled through water.

Working with mercury was what led Priestley to his greatest discovery. When mercury is strongly heated in air, a brick-red powder forms on its surface. This is the result of its combining with a portion of the air. Priestley collected this red powder, placed it in a jar, and heated it strongly with the concentrated sunlight produced by a magnifying lens.

The powder broke down into mercury again, releasing the portion of the air with which it had earlier combined. The mercury collected as small metallic droplets while the released air spread through the jar as an invisible vapor.

The mercury had combined with what was only a minor constituent of the air. In giving it off again, it produced the gas in pure form and Priestley was able to observe its curious properties. When he placed a smoldering splint into a jar filled with this gas, the splint promptly burst into bright flame, which it would not have done if the gas had been merely air. This property of the new gas was precisely the opposite of that of Rutherford's gas, in which the smoldering splint (or even a brightly-burning one) would have gone out at once.

Priestley was fascinated by this new gas. He found that mice placed in a closed bell-jar containing this gas were unusually frisky and that he himself when he breathed it felt "light and easy."

He did not, however, understand what it was he had discovered, any more than Rutherford had. That privilege fell to another, a French chemist, Antoine Laurent Lavoisier. By 1775, Lavoisier had come to the conclusion that air is made up principally of two gases. One-fifth of it is Priestley's gas, which encourages combustion, and four-fifths is Rutherford's gas, which will not permit combustion.

Lavoisier named Priestley's gas "oxygen" from Greek words meaning "acid-producer" because he believed that all acids contained it. He was wrong there for some acids do not contain oxygen; nevertheless, the name persists.

Rutherford's gas he named "azote" from Greek words meaning "no life" because mice placed in a container of azote died. Apparently, oxygen was not only necessary for burning, but it was also necessary for the life processes of the body. To Lavoisier it seemed there must be a very slow kind of burning that went on in the body, too, a burning that supplied the energy for life. This slow internal burning is called "respiration" and oxygen is necessary for it, while azote will not permit it, if it alone is present.

The name, azote, did not stick, and the gas came to be called "nitrogen" instead ("niter-producing") because it could be obtained from a common mineral called "niter."

Actually, we now know that air is about 78 per cent nitrogen and 21 per cent oxygen. This adds up only to 99 per cent, you will notice. That is because the remaining 1 per cent is made up of a mixture of gases that are neither oxygen nor nitrogen. Most of these were not discovered till the 1890's,* and they don't need to concern us here.

The only gaseous component of air, other than nitrogen and oxygen, which we ought to mention is carbon dioxide, which Black had earlier discovered to exist there. It is only a minor component indeed, making up something like 0.035 per cent of the air, but, as we shall see, it is of crucial importance to life on Earth.

Lavoisier reasoned that the process of burning involved the combination of the burning object with the oxygen (and only the oxygen) of the air. Take coal, for instance. It is made up of a substance that chemists call "carbon" (taken from the Latin word for coal). When coal burns, the carbon that makes it up combines with the oxygen and forms the gas, carbon dioxide.

The gas receives its name, indeed, because it is formed of a certain combination of carbon and oxygen. It was Lavoisier him-

---

* These gases, though irrelevant to this book, have a fascinating history of their own, which you can follow in my book *The Noble Gases* (New York: Basic Books, 1966).

self, with the aid of a number of colleagues, who worked up this system of naming substances by building on the names of the simpler substances that combined to form them.

The simplest substances (so simple that they can be broken down to nothing simpler) we now called "elements"; the more complex substances formed out of the elements are called "compounds." Carbon dioxide is a compound formed out of the two elements, carbon and oxygen.

There is another simple and important case of an element combining with oxygen; one that involves an inflammable gas that had been observed by both Van Helmont and Hales. It was first studied in detail, however, in 1766 by an English chemist, Henry Cavendish. In 1784, he allowed it to burn in air, trapped the resulting vapors and discovered they condensed to form water.

When Lavoisier heard of this experiment, he repeated it and gave the inflammable gas the name of "hydrogen" ("water producer"). Lavoisier saw that the combination of hydrogen and oxygen formed water. Properly water ought to be called "hydrogen monoxide" but, of course, nothing can replace the old, familiar name for that substance.

Lavoisier made the first crude chemical analysis of substances obtained from food and it seemed plain to him that the complex food-stuffs were rich in carbon and hydrogen. Oxygen, taken into the body by way of the lungs, made contact with the food. Carbon and hydrogen combined with the oxygen slowly to form carbon dioxide and water.

To Lavoisier the combination of a substance with oxygen was a case of "oxidation." Sometimes the oxygen did not combine with the substance directly, but combined with some of the hydrogen contained in the substance. For that reason we can consider oxidation to be either the addition of oxygen to a substance, or the subtraction of hydrogen from it.*

When oxidation takes place rapidly, we have the process we

* Nowadays, chemists have a far more sophisticated way of looking at oxidation, but this rather old-fashioned definition will suit our purposes perfectly and will have the advantage of not introducing unnecessary complexities.

ordinarily refer to as burning. Rapid oxidation produces energy which is poured into the surrounding environment. We are perfectly aware of this for we detect it in burning objects as heat and light.

Oxidation within the body ("respiration") takes place much more slowly and, it is reasonable to suppose, produces energy much more slowly. Nevertheless it produces a mild heat in warmblooded animals, and in some creatures it produces dim light. The energy that is produced in this slow oxidation is carefully husbanded by the body and makes possible all the energy-consuming processes (movement, for instance) that we associate with life.

We can summarize this in the following equation:

$$\text{food} + \text{oxygen} \xrightarrow{\text{(respiration)}} \text{carbon dioxide} + \text{water} + \text{energy}$$

(Equation 1)

Eliminating the Superfluous

As you see now, we are back to the two problems I set at the start of the book. Food and oxygen are consumed in the course of respiration. Why, then, don't we run out of them?

The food is somehow produced again by plants: from the soil (according to the ancients), or from the water (according to Van Helmont) or even possibly from the air (according to Hales). But where does the oxygen come from? How is it restored to the air?

The first hint at an answer came from Priestley, the discoverer of oxygen. He, too, like Rutherford, experimented with an enclosed batch of air in which a candle had burned and which could no longer support either burning or life (because, as we now know, the oxygen had been consumed). Priestley put a mouse in the enclosed air and it quickly died. He then thought he would try a bit of plant life, too. If burned-out air didn't support life, it ought not to support life in any form. Plants ought not be supported any more than animals. Priestley therefore put a sprig of mint into a glass of water and put it into the enclosed air.

The little plant did *not* die. It grew there for months and seemed to flourish. What was more, at the end of that time, a mouse could be placed in the enclosed air and it would live—and a candle would burn.

Priestley did not properly interpret these results because neither then, nor afterward, did he adopt Lavoisier's view of the matter. From Lavoisier's viewpoint, however, what had happened was that whereas the original burning candle had removed the oxygen from the air, the plant had restored the oxygen!

Apparently, the world of plant life not only constantly restores the food supply of the plant, but it also restores the oxygen supply as well.

A Dutch physician, Jan Ingenhousz, heard of Priestley's experiment and was on fire to go more deeply into the matter. In 1779, he performed many experiments on this restorative effect of plants, and made a momentous discovery. He found that plants produced their oxygen only in the presence of sunlight; never at night.

It seems reasonable to suspect that the plant forms both food and oxygen as part of the same process. In forming food, complex substances are formed from simple substances in the soil, water or air. Chemists call the process of putting together complex substances from simple ones "synthesis" from Greek words meaning "to put together." Since sunlight is essential to oxygen production and therefore to food synthesis the process is called "photosynthesis" ("to put together by light"). We might say, then, that Ingenhousz discovered photosynthesis.

But if food and oxygen are formed, out of what are they formed? A Swiss minister, Jean Senebier, conducted experiments which led him, in 1782, to agree with Ingenhousz that light was essential to oxygen-production, and to argue further that something else was necessary, too—carbon dioxide. Oxygen would not be evolved if the plant were deprived of all contact with carbon dioxide, either as gas in the air or in solution (as "bicarbonate") in water.

In 1804, another Swiss scholar, Nicolas Theodore de Saussure, went about matters quantitatively. Indeed, he tried Van Helmont's experiment all over again, but with carbon dioxide in mind, rather than soil. That is, he carefully measured how much carbon dioxide was used up by a plant and how much weight of tissue it gained. The gain in tissue weight was considerably greater than the weight of carbon dioxide used up and de Saussure showed quite convincingly that the only possible source of the remaining weight was water.

So it seemed that both Van Helmont and Hales were each, in their way, at least partly right. Plants are nourished by both the water and by a portion of the air and draw part of their tissue substance from each.

We can see this to be necessary from the new Lavoisier view of chemistry. Food contains carbon and hydrogen and must therefore be formed out of simpler materials, containing carbon and hydrogen. (The elements, by Lavoisier's view, could neither be created nor destroyed, a rule that is called the "law of conservation of matter.")*

We know that water is made up of hydrogen and oxygen, and we know that carbon dioxide is made up of carbon and oxygen. Both water and carbon dioxide are always available to plants and it seems reasonable, then, that they should contribute to the formation of food; that is, of plant tissue. Furthermore, if the carbon of carbon dioxide and the hydrogen of water are used to form food, then the oxygen left over would be expelled into the atmosphere.

But can we eliminate the soil altogether? Remember that some minor soil components are necessary to plant life and, as a matter

---

* This rule is not quite correct, as was discovered at the beginning of the twentieth century, but it is precise enough for the purposes of this book.

of fact, plant tissues do not consist of carbon, hydrogen and oxygen only. These three elements do indeed make up some 95 per cent of the tissue weight but there are other elements present as well; elements that, in their smaller quantities, are nevertheless absolutely essential to life. These include nitrogen, sulfur, phosphorus, calcium, magnesium, iron, sodium, potassium and several others.

If we put nitrogen to one side for the moment we can see that none of the other elements are to be found in significant quantities in the air or in rain. There are, however, compounds containing these elements in the soil. Water washing through the soil will dissolve some of these compounds and they will then enter the plant with the water. Water is necessary to plant life, then, not merely as a source of plant tissue, but as a transport of soil compounds.

So you see, the soil does its part as well. The minor constituents of soil that are necessary to plant life are returned to the soil when plants die and slowly decay. If plants are eaten, some of the material is returned in the form of animal waste and the rest when the animal dies and decays.

It is only when man cultivates the soil intensively and then reaps the plant life and carts it away, that the soil is slowly depleted of these substances and grows barren. Farmers must then restore these substances by fertilizing it with animal wastes or with special chemical fertilizers developed over the last century.

These substances of the soil are incorporated into plant tissue by mechanisms that don't involve the action of sunlight, and are not part of photosynthesis. In this book, we are concentrating on the process of photosynthesis and on matters directly relating to it. We will therefore eliminate the superfluous and avoid any discussion of the soil substances except where some direct connection is found.

The same is true, for that matter, in connection with respiration. If we consider the breakdown of food to carbon dioxide and water, that takes into account the elements, carbon, hydrogen and oxygen only. What about the other elements undoubtedly present in food? We are not (photosynthetically speaking) concerned with them and so we will ignore them.

Nitrogen is the doubtful case. Next to carbon, hydrogen and oxygen, nitrogen is the most common element found in living tissue generally, animal as well as plant. It is a vital part of the most important of the compounds of living tissue: the proteins and the nucleic acids. And nitrogen is present in the air. Indeed, four-fifths of the air is nitrogen.

It would seem reasonable, therefore, to suspect that air contributes to plant nourishment by means of its nitrogen content as well as by its tiny carbon dioxide content, and that nitrogen plays a part in photosynthesis.

The first to conduct experiments in this connection was a French agricultural chemist, Jean Baptiste Boussingault. Beginning in 1837, he prepared soil which contained no nitrogen compounds and grew weighed amounts of seed in it. He was careful to allow no nitrogen-containing substances to reach the growing plants, so that if they gained nitrogen, that could come only from the atmosphere.

He found that some plants did indeed grow under such nitrogen-free conditions. Peas and red clover not only grew and flourished but their tissues were as rich in nitrogen as were plants that grew in nitrogen-containing soil. Peas and clover had clearly obtained their nitrogen from the atmosphere.

Yet Boussingault also found that other plants, such as wheat and barley, would not grow at all under nitrogen-free conditions.

This remained a puzzle until the mid-nineteenth century when bacteria came to be studied in detail and their importance in the economy of life generally became increasingly well understood.

It turned out that there were certain bacteria which could make use of the nitrogen of the air, turning it into compounds like those often found in soil. Such bacteria tended to grow in nodules that attached themselves to the roots of certain plants, notably peas, beans and clover. The bacteria formed nitrogen compounds in quantities greater than they themselves required and the plants absorbed the excess. Peas, beans and clover did not make use of atmospheric nitrogen directly, but only after the bacteria had done their work. If these plants were grown in soil that was not only nitrogen-free, but sterile and bacteria-free, then they could not grow any longer.

This means that we can eliminate nitrogen, too, from our consideration of photosynthesis. No plants can utilize it directly from the atmosphere and it plays no direct role in photosynthesis.

Completing the Cycle

Now we are left, for the while, with three elements only: carbon, hydrogen and oxygen.

Just as we summarized the facts of respiration in Equation 1, let us find a way for summarizing the facts of photosynthesis. We start with carbon dioxide and water and we end with plant tissue and oxygen. We are interested in plant tissue at the moment chiefly as food, so let's call it food. Then, too, let us remember that sunlight is essential and that sunlight is a form of energy; so let's add energy as one of the inputs. We then have:

$$\text{energy} + \text{water} + \text{carbon dioxide} \xrightarrow{\text{(photosynthesis)}} \text{oxygen} + \text{food}$$

$$(Equation\ 2)$$

If we compare Equations 1 and 2, we find that one is the precise opposite of the other.

In other words, if we consider oxygen and food on one side and carbon dioxide, water and energy on the other side, then we see that respiration pushes everything to the carbon dioxide, water, energy side, while photosynthesis pushes everything to the food, oxygen side.

This is what we mean when we speak of a cycle. Equations 1 and 2 can therefore be combined to form what is called the "carbon cycle" because the element carbon seems to play a key role in it (though one that is actually no more vital than that played by hydrogen and oxygen, and—as we shall eventually see—by certain other elements as well).

Before presenting the cycle, however, let's clarify a few points. Respiration takes place both in animals and plants, even though the process is less apparent in plants, which do not visibly breathe. In the sunlight, the effect of photosynthesis masks that of respiration in the plant; at night, however, when photosynthesis does not take place, plants absorb oxygen and give off carbon dioxide just as animals do, as was first shown, in 1868, by the German botanist, Julius von Sachs. (On the whole, though, photosynthesis is the dominant reaction in plants, so that there is a net production of oxygen. Plant respiration does *not* cancel out plant photosynthesis, far from it.)

Photosynthesis, however, takes place only in plants, never in animals. (There are certain bacteria which display chemical reactions very like photosynthesis.)

Another point is that Equations 1 and 2 are not precise opposites in every respect. In respiration, the energy produced is partly given off as heat and is partly stored in the form of certain compounds. We can speak of the energy that is made available by the breakdown of these compounds as "chemical energy." It is this chemical energy which is particularly vital to life, so let us for the moment ignore the fact that heat is also produced and refer to the energy produced in respiration as chemical energy and nothing more.

In photosynthesis, however, the energy that is made use of is neither ordinary heat nor chemical energy. It is the energy of sunlight, which we may call "solar energy."

With that in mind, let us now write a combination of Equations 1 and 2, in the form of a cycle—see Figure 1.

Here is the great cycle that keeps life going indefinitely. If it works perfectly food, oxygen, carbon dioxide and water are used up and formed, used up and formed, over and over again, and can in theory last forever.

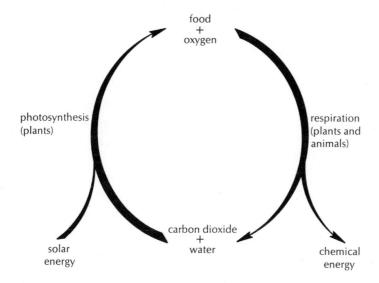

Figure 1. The Carbon Cycle

What drives the cycle (as we shall see in detail in this book) is sunlight and we might say that the whole "purpose" of the cycle is to convert solar energy into chemical energy. (This was first pointed out, by the way, in 1845, by a German physician, Julius Robert von Mayer.)

It is chemical energy that makes possible all the manifestations of life, and since its source is solar energy, all of life (ourselves included) depends upon the Sun for everything. And it is plants, through photosynthesis, that make the energy of sunlight available not only to themselves but to all animals as well.

2

The Members of the Cycle

Sharpening the Vague

We have now answered the problem posed at the beginning of the book and can see why food and oxygen are not used up. The answer, however, is given in only the broadest and vaguest possible terms. There are no details, and surely we would like all the details we can get concerning a cycle on which all life depends.

The vaguest of all the terms used in Figure 1, our first representation of the carbon cycle, is "food." Mankind eats a variety of kinds of food. Indeed, almost everything non-poisonous that can be chewed, swallowed, and used as nourishment, has served as food for some group of men or other. It would be useful if we could sharpen that particularly vague term.

All the wide variety of food can be boiled down to three classes of substances that together make up the major portion of all the edible food in existence. There are 1) "carbohydrates," 2) "lipids" or, more commonly, "fat," and 3) "proteins."

These have a variety of uses in the body, but we are not concerned with most of those uses. The carbon cycle is a method for using and producing energy, so we would be interested in knowing if one of these classes of foodstuffs is more concerned with energy-production than the others.

As a matter of fact, each of the three types of substances can be used as a source of energy, but not with equal readiness. Proteins, for instance, are the key substances of living tissue. They exist in thousands of forms and perform thousands of vital functions. Although they can be used for the production of energy, this happens only in desperate circumstances, or when necessary to get rid of some surplus. It is not the routine body fuel anymore than furniture is the routine fire-place fuel (though chairs may be used, in desperation, when firewood is not available).

The "firewood" in the case of living tissue are the carbohydrates and fat. Of the two, fat represents the more concentrated store of energy. That is, an ounce of fat, combining with oxygen, will produce more energy than an ounce of carbohydrate will. Fat, therefore, is a more economical way of storing large quantities of energy. (An obese person would be at least twice as bulky if his over-large energy store were to be present as carbohydrate rather than fat.)

Fat is useful as an energy-store for another reason. It is insoluble in water. Living tissue is very watery (some four-fifths of its weight is water) and the chemical reactions that take place in it generally take place in association with this water. By its insolubility, fat is, so to speak, withdrawn from the chemical hurly-burly within the tissues to a large extent. A large bulk of it can be stored away without its getting in the way of the busy chemical machinery of the body.

The very insolubility of fat, however, means it can be drawn upon only with some trouble. Carbohydrates, which are much more compatible with water, can be used on shorter notice and with fewer complications.

To be sure, carbohydrates occur in many forms and some of them are as insoluble in water as fat is, and are even more intractable. One type of carbohydrate is "cellulose," which is used by plants as a supporting structure. Wood is largely cellulose.

Neither plants nor animals can use cellulose for energy productions. Termites and certain other insects live on wood, to be sure, but this is possible only because there are microscopic creatures ("microorganisms") in their digestive tract, and these are capable of breaking down cellulose. Simple products are thus produced which can be used for energy, and in quantities more than enough for the needs of the microorganisms themselves. The termite gets the overflow.

In the same way, cattle and other ruminants obtain their nourishment from grass and other plant life high in cellulose. Bacteria in the digestive tract break down the cellulose and only so is it possible for cattle to live on such a diet.

Another complex form of carbohydrate which is insoluble in water is "starch." This does not form strong fibers as cellulose does, but exists rather as powdery grains.

Both cellulose and starch are built up from a particular chemical unit hooked together in long chains. Indeed, both are built up of the *same* unit; it is just that the interconnections in the case of cellulose resist breakage by the chemical mechanisms available to plants and animals, whereas the interconnections in the case of starch are easy to break.

Any animal possesses the ability to break down starch in its digestive tract. The units out of which it is built up then exist free and isolated, and can be absorbed into the body and used for energy. This unit is called "glucose."

Glucose can still be classified as a carbohydrate, but as a very simple one. Simple carbohydrates are called "sugars" and glucose is distinguished from other sugars by the fact that it was early discovered in grapes, so that it is sometimes called "grape sugar."

In the human body, there are ample supplies of fat, but the energy store that is subject to instant call is "glycogen," a form of starch stored in the liver and muscles.

When energy is required, glycogen is easily converted into its glucose units. (Indeed, the very name, glycogen, derives from Greek words meaning "glucose producer.") The glucose so produced is diffused into the blood, and the blood stream carries it to all parts of the body.

It is glucose, then, that is the immediate food supply of human tissue. The body economy is such that the glucose content of the blood is maintained at a very steady value, despite variations in the food intake and in energy consumption. Because of this, glucose can be called "blood sugar" as well as grape sugar.

What is true of human tissue is true of living tissue generally. Glucose is a key compound from the standpoint of energy production. Furthermore, chemists have, in the last half-century, worked out more and more of the details of the chemical mechanisms taking place within tissue. Under the proper circumstances, glucose can be converted into almost any other tissue substance and vice versa. It seems completely fair to let glucose stand for food substances generally and consider it as the representative energy source.

In other words, we can sharpen the equation for respiration (see Equation 1 on page 18) by substituting "glucose" for "food." This gives us:

$$\text{glucose} + \text{oxygen} \xrightarrow{\text{(respiration)}} \text{carbon dioxide} + \text{water} + \text{energy}$$

(*Equation 3*)

However, we are dealing with a cycle now and we can't make any substitution in one half of it, unless we are sure those substitutions will fit the other half as well. Can we use glucose in place of food in connection with photosynthesis too, in other words?

The key experiment here was carried through by Sachs, the discoverer of plant respiration (see page 24). He knew that plant leaves, under normal conditions, contained starch. This is easy to demonstrate, for starch reacts with iodine to form a black substance, and if leaves are exposed to the vapor of iodine, they turn black. If, however, leaves are kept in the dark for some hours, they consume their own starch for energy purposes and no longer react with iodine vapor.

In 1872, Sachs placed such a starch-depleted leaf in the sunlight, but covered half of it with an opaque cover. After some time, Sachs exposed all of the leaf to iodine vapor. The half that had been in sunlight turned black; the other half, which had been kept in darkness, did not.

It seemed clear, then, that photosynthesis had produced starch in the leaf (rather than some other substance such as fat or protein). Since starch is built up of long strings of glucose units hooked together, it seems reasonable to suppose that glucose is formed first, and is then combined to form starch.

We would seem justified, then, in substituting glucose for food in the photosynthesis portion of the cycle, as well as in the respiration portion. The entire cycle can therefore be rewritten as in Figure 2.

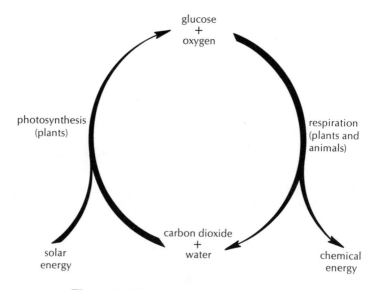

Figure 2. The Carbon Cycle (with Glucose)

Listing the Atoms

The substitution of "glucose" for "food" is more than the mere replacement of a vague term by a sharp one. Food is a vast and complex mixture of a large variety of different substances, and chemists cannot possibly treat such a mixture as a unit. Glucose, on the other hand, is a single well-defined substance that the chemist can handle, study, and discuss without trouble.

The ease with which glucose, as a chemical compound, can be dealt with arises, in part at least, out of the fact that in the first decades of the nineteenth century, chemists worked out a convenient "language." They developed methods of indicating the chemical nature of the various compounds by a set of rational symbols made possible by the fact that, beginning in 1803, the English chemist, John Dalton, had developed an "atomic theory" of matter.

Dalton maintained that all matter was made up of tiny particles, far too small to be seen even in the best microscope. These he called "atoms." Each element was made up of a different variety of atom. Thus carbon was made up of "carbon atoms," hydrogen of "hydrogen atoms" and oxygen of "oxygen atoms."

These atoms might exist singly, but usually they clung together in groups. These atom-groups are called "molecules" and chemists found that they could best define a substance by working out the number and kinds of atoms within such a molecule.

As an example, oxygen, as it occurs in the atmosphere, consists of molecules, each of which is made up of two oxygen atoms clinging together. Atoms of different types might also cling together. For instance, two hydrogen atoms and an oxygen atom cling together to form a molecule of water. One carbon atom and two oxygen atoms cling together to form a molecule of carbon dioxide.

Instead of giving a compound a name (which may or may not be descriptive of its structure) it is possible to use symbols to indicate the number and kinds of atoms that make up the molecules of the compound.

The system used is to represent an atom of each element by a letter (or sometimes by two letters). In the case of carbon, hydrogen, and oxygen, the letters used are, conveniently enough, the initial letters of the names of the element. Thus, a carbon atom is represented by C, a hydrogen atom by H and an oxygen atom by O. These letters are the "chemical symbols" of the elements.

If there is more than one atom of a particular kind in a compound, the number of atoms is represented by the appropriate subscript; that is, small digits written below the line. Thus, since the oxygen molecule contains two oxygen atoms, it can be written O_2. This is the "chemical formula" of oxygen.

What might be referred to as "oxygen in the form occurring in the atmosphere" or "atmospheric oxygen" or even "molecular oxygen" can be written, much more conveniently and concisely, as O_2. Furthermore, O_2 gives us more information than any of the alternate phrases. When we write O_2, we see at once that there are two oxygen atoms in the molecule, and this can be vitally important to a chemist studying a chemical reaction. He might conceivably forget the two-atom situation if he spoke always of "oxygen," but he couldn't possibly do so if he spoke of O_2.

The carbon dioxide molecule, made up of one carbon atom and two oxygen atoms, can be written CO_2, and the water molecule, made up of two hydrogen atoms and an oxygen atom, can be written H_2O. It so happens that the name, carbon dioxide, is a good one since it indicates the presence of one carbon and two oxygen atoms, if you happen to know that the prefix "di-" means "two." The name "water," however, is completely uninformative and is a poor substitute indeed for H_2O.

We might therefore write the respiration reaction (see Equation 3 on page 29) much more concisely and informatively as:

$$\text{glucose} + O_2 \xrightarrow{\text{(respiration)}} CO_2 + H_2O + \text{energy}$$

(Equation 4)

But that brings us to glucose. Can that, too, be represented as a chemical formula? It is easy to see that since all compounds are built up of molecules which are in turn made up of atoms, all compounds can be presented as chemical formulas. What is theoretically possible, however, can be impractical in reality.

The complex substances of living tissue belong to a group

called "organic compounds" because they are to be found in living organisms rather than in the mineral world. Whereas oxygen, carbon dioxide and water have molecules made up of two or three atoms apiece, organic compounds have molecules containing dozens of atoms, hundreds, thousands, even millions. The simple molecules of the mineral world ("inorganic compound") can usually be expressed as formulas with very little trouble. Not so the complex organic molecules where the problem of the exact structure of the larger members is only now being slowly solved.

Starch, for instance, is made up of giant molecules in numberless variations and if it were starch that was a part of our carbon cycle, we would be unable to find a true and complete formula for it (although we could use a simplified formula that would do well enough).

Glucose, however (and fortunately), is one of the simpler organic compounds, with molecules made up of a mere two dozen atoms. The exact number and nature of these atoms was worked out in 1868, when the German chemist, Rudolf Fittig, established the glucose molecule to be made up of six carbon atoms, twelve hydrogen atoms, and six oxygen atoms. It can therefore be written thus: $C_6H_{12}O_6$.

Suppose now we want to write the respiration equation by making use of the chemical formula for glucose. We would have to say that $C_6H_{12}O_6$ plus O_2 forms CO_2 and H_2O. But the glucose molecule contains six carbon atoms while the carbon dioxide molecule contains only one. Each one of the six carbon atoms in the glucose molecule can be made part of a separate carbon dioxide molecule. A glucose molecule would therefore have to give rise to six carbon dioxide molecules, which we can write as $6CO_2$. Similarly, the twelve hydrogen atoms of the glucose molecule can move, by pairs, into water molecules. There would be six pairs altogether and so six water molecules would be formed—$6H_2O$.

If a glucose molecule gives rise to $6CO_2$ and $6H_2O$, then those molecules have eighteen oxygen atoms altogether (twelve in the six carbon dioxide molecules plus six in the six water molecules). Where do all these oxygen atoms come from? The glucose molecule, itself, has six oxygen atoms, which means that twelve more are needed.

This is where the oxygen from the air comes in. Since this oxygen occurs in the form of molecules made up of two oxygen atoms each, the twelve oxygen atoms must be supplied in the form of six oxygen molecules; that is, $6O_2$. We can therefore express the respiration reaction (see Equation 4 on page 32) as follows:

$$C_6H_{12}O_6 + 6O_2 \xrightarrow{\text{(respiration)}} 6CO_2 + 6H_2O + \text{energy}$$

(*Equation 5*)

If you compare the part of the equation on the left side of the arrow with the part on the right side, you will see there is an atomic balance. There are, altogether, 6 carbon atoms, 12 hydrogen atoms and 18 oxygen atoms on the left side; and there are, altogether, 6 carbon atoms, 12 hydrogen atoms and 18 oxygen atoms on the right side. This is an example of a "balanced chemical equation" and all equations should be balanced. In chemical processes, atoms do not disappear into nothingness, nor do they appear from nothingness.

Arranging the Atoms

Suppose we take a closer look at the formula of glucose, $C_6H_{12}O_6$. The $H_{12}O_6$ looks as though it might represent six water molecules, $6H_2O$. Could one then write the glucose molecules as $C_6(H_2O)_6$; that is, as a string of six carbon atoms with a water molecule attached to each one?

When the formulas of glucose and other sugars were being worked out, there were some suspicions that this might be so. Indeed, the very term "carbohydrate" arose out of this suspicion. It means in Graeco-Latin "watered-carbon."

But it is *not* so. I mention the suspicion only because it accounts for the name of the class of compounds to which glucose belongs and because it had some influence on the development of ideas about photosynthesis. Actually, there are no water molecules in the glucose molecule, as was eventually found out.

In order to demonstrate the presence or absence of water molecules within a larger molecule, chemists had to be able to work out not only the number and kind of atoms within a molecule but the exact manner in which they were arranged. This began to become possible in 1850, when the English chemist, Edward Frankland, first demonstrated that a particular type of atom could form linkages with a fixed number of other atoms. This notion was further developed and applied to organic compounds particularly by the German chemist Friedrich August Kekulé in 1858.

To see how this works, let us for the moment confine ourselves to the three kinds of atoms that primarily interest us just now: carbon, hydrogen and oxygen. A carbon atom can attach itself to as many as four other atoms by connecting links called "bonds"; an oxygen atom to as many as two; and a hydrogen atom only to one.

We can emphasize this characteristic number of bonds per atom (the so-called "valence" of an element) by adding to the symbol of the element the number of bonds it possesses in the form of short dashes:

$$-\overset{\displaystyle |}{\underset{\displaystyle |}{C}}- \qquad -O- \qquad H-$$

Such atoms can join together to form molecules where each atom uses one of its bonds for connection with a neighboring atom; or sometimes two; or, very occasionally if it has enough, three.

For instance, the oxygen molecule, the carbon dioxide molecule and the water molecule, can be written to show the manner of connection and the number of connecting bonds in such a way as to show a "structural formula."*

O=O   O=C=O   H—O—H
oxygen   carbon   water
                       dioxide

Notice that in such formulas the number of bonds ending at the hydrogen atom is always one, at the oxygen atom two, and at the carbon atom four.

In the case of such simple molecules, not much is gained by putting down the structural formulas. To the practiced chemist, the arrangements shown here are virtually second nature, and it is quite sufficient to continue saying O_2, CO_2 and H_2O. That also goes for other molecules made up of half a dozen atoms or less.

Not so in the case of organic compounds with their numerous atoms. There the structural formulas are much more helpful than the simple "empirical formulas" which, as in the case of $C_6H_{12}O_6$, merely count the total number of each kind of atom. This is particularly so, since a particular number of particular kinds of atoms can often be arranged in more than one way, each arrangement giving rise to a different compound with different properties, although the same empirical formula holds for all. Three comparatively simple examples of what I mean are given in Figure 3—three pairs of "isomers."

Even for the simple substances shown in Figure 3, structural formulas are clearly necessary to distinguish between compounds, which cannot be distinguished by empirical formulas alone. For really complicated compounds, the number of possible arrangements can easily reach into the millions, and there just isn't any way to do without structural formulas.

Naturally, chemists do what they can to simplify such formulas. Usually, they attempt to avoid sticking numerous hydrogen atoms at the end of bonds like so many porcupine quills. It is assumed that the person who must work with formulas quickly learns how to

* The structural formulas shown in this book are the simplest possible. Modern chemical theory introduces certain refinements that are essential if molecular properties are to be entirely explained, but these need not concern us in this book.

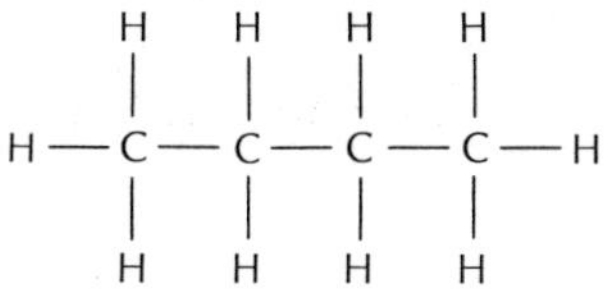

butane (C$_4$H$_{10}$)

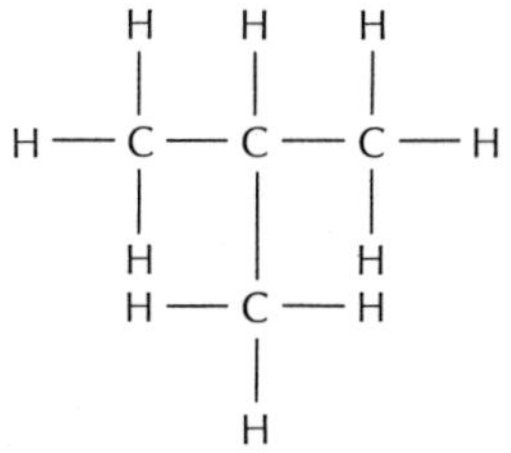

isobutane (C$_4$H$_{10}$)

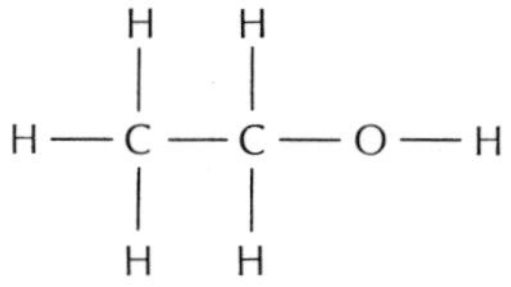

ethyl alcohol (C$_2$H$_6$O)

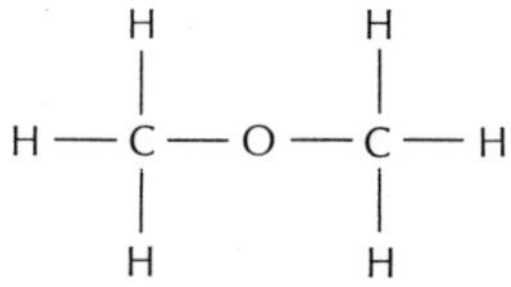

dimethyl ether (C$_2$H$_6$O)

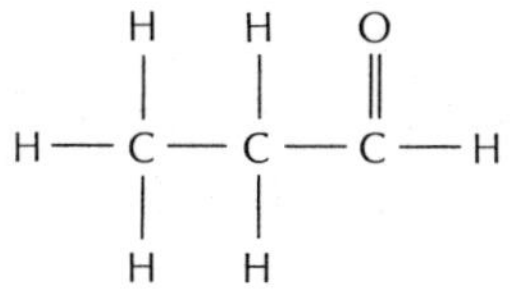

propionaldehyde (C$_3$H$_6$O)

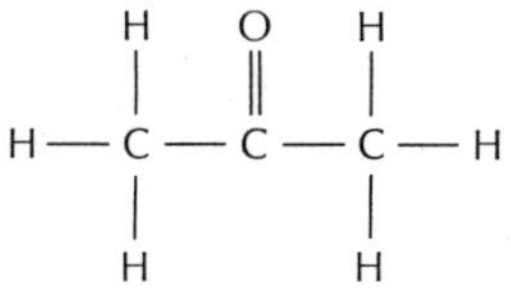

acetone (C$_3$H$_6$O)

Figure 3. Pairs of Isomers

assign the correct number of bonds to each atom and how to arrange the hydrogen atoms properly. Leaving this to be done "in the head" so to speak, one can then concentrate on the arrangement of the remaining atoms. Other shortcuts can also be taken, but in this book, I will take no further liberties with the reader. I will merely pull in the hydrogen atoms and condense no more.

The formulas given, in full, in Figure 3, can be presented in this condensed form in Figure 4. I suspect that you will agree, on

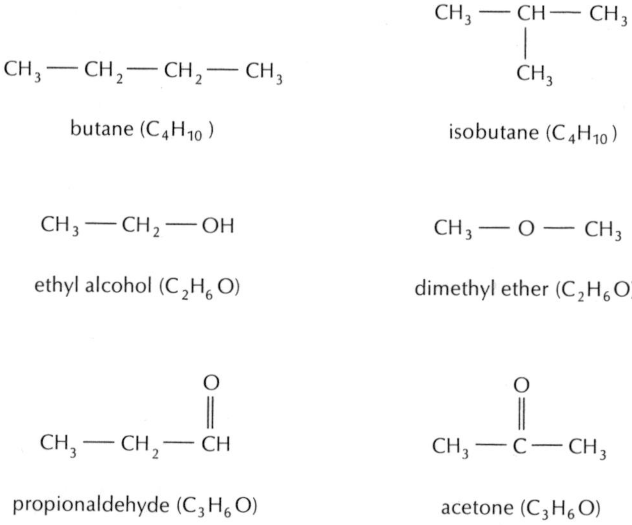

$$CH_3 - CH_2 - CH_2 - CH_3$$

butane (C_4H_{10})

$$CH_3 - CH - CH_3$$
$$|$$
$$CH_3$$

isobutane (C_4H_{10})

$$CH_3 - CH_2 - OH$$

ethyl alcohol (C_2H_6O)

$$CH_3 - O - CH_3$$

dimethyl ether (C_2H_6O)

$$\overset{\displaystyle O}{\overset{\|}{CH_3 - CH_2 - CH}}$$

propionaldehyde (C_3H_6O)

$$\overset{\displaystyle O}{\overset{\|}{CH_3 - C - CH_3}}$$

acetone (C_3H_6O)

Figure 4. Pairs of Isomers (Condensed Formulas)

comparing Figure 4 with Figure 3, that nothing is lost in condensing the formulas and that, indeed, by condensing them there is a gain. The differences between the isomers, and the essential arrangements of the atoms, are made plainer by pulling in the hydrogen atoms.

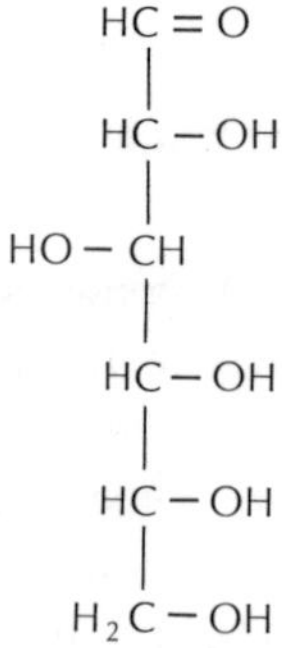

$$HC = O$$
$$|$$
$$HC - OH$$
$$|$$
$$HO - CH$$
$$|$$
$$HC - OH$$
$$|$$
$$HC - OH$$
$$|$$
$$H_2C - OH$$

glucose ($C_6H_{12}O_6$)

Figure 5. Glucose

It was not till 1891 that the structural formula of glucose was worked out by the German chemist Emil Fischer. There are many ways of presenting this structural formula and of the alternatives I shall present the simplest in Figure 5. The formula shown there is inaccurate in that it represents the six carbon atoms in a straight line where, in actual fact, five carbon atoms plus one of the oxygen atoms form a six-membered ring. Nevertheless, for the purposes of this book, this "straight-chain" formula is sufficient. It is easier to handle and visualize than the ring formula, and will display those properties of glucose we will have to deal with.

You may wonder why one of the hydrogen-oxygen atom combinations (which we may call a "hydroxyl group" and write either "OH" or "HO") is made to point to the left in the glucose formula, while the others point to the right. This results from the fact that the atom-arrangement within molecules is really distributed through three dimensions. In presenting the formulas on a sheet of paper, in two dimensions, we are forced to make certain conventional decisions concerning left and right.

There are three other common sugars, for instance, called fructose, galactose and mannose. Each has the empirical formula $C_6H_{12}O_6$, like glucose. Each can be represented with a six-carbon chain to which are attached five hydroxyl groups and one doubly-bound oxygen ($=O$). The differences lie in the three-dimensional arrangement of the hydroxyl groups about the carbon atoms and this is shown in two-dimensional formulas by altering the distribution of those hydroxyl compounds to right and left. Glucose is the only substance of its type which we shall have to deal with so deeply as to need a structural formula; let us then go no further into the subject but accept its hydroxyl group arrangement as given.

Now take another look at the glucose formula. You will see that there are no water molecules, as such, in it. The water molecule is made up of a hydrogen atom attached to a hydroxyl group (H—OH). In the glucose molecule there are a number of hydrogen atoms and a number of hydroxyl groups but in no case are these attached to each other. In every case, hydrogen atoms and hydroxyl groups are separately attached to carbon atoms. A hydrogen atom and a hydroxyl group may be attached to the same carbon atom, but that is as close as they get to each other and that is not close enough to make water.

Now that this is clear, let us see if we can use this appreciation of glucose structure to simplify the respiration equation (Equation 5 on page 34). It is a little complicated to have to deal with six molecules each, of oxygen, carbon dioxide and water, for the sake of balancing the equation, yet if we deal with the intact six-carbon glucose molecules we have to. Why not, then, deal with one-sixth of a glucose molecule?

If we deal with the empirical formula only, the temptation is strong to present the matter almost as though it were an exercise in arithmetic.

$$\frac{C_6H_{12}O_6}{6} = CH_2O$$

Before the importance of structural formulas was properly understood, such an arithmetical exercise could be given more weight than it was worth. The empirical formula CH_2O represents "formaldehyde." The formula might, more properly, be written $H_2C{=}O$, but it seems scarcely worth while doing so since the molecule is so simple. There is only one way to arrange one carbon atom, two hydrogen atoms and one oxygen atom in such a way as to give a legitimate compound and that one way is formaldehyde.

The temptation is almost overwhelming to decide that one-sixth of a glucose molecule is formaldehyde.

Even before Sachs had definitely proved (in 1872) the production of starch through photosynthesis, many had assumed starch to be the product. They had gone on to make the logical assumption that since starch was built up of glucose units, it was glucose that was first formed in photosynthesis and that many glucose molecules were then combined to form starch.

In 1870, the German chemist Adolf Baeyer went an apparently logical step farther. Should not photosynthesis form formaldehyde first? Six formaldehyde molecules would combine to form one glucose and many glucose molecules would then combine to form starch. Formaldehyde could indeed be made to combine into sugar-like substances so that Baeyer's theory seemed fairly plausible.

To be sure, no one could demonstrate this sort of formaldehyde combination in living tissue, or even detect formaldehyde there doing anything at all. Yet it was easy to suspect that formaldehyde might be used up so quickly after formation that the amount present at any instant would be too little to detect.

For three-quarters of a century, the formaldehyde hypothesis held on to life. It was only in recent times that it was disproved, through experiments to be described later in this book.

I hesitate, then, to write the formula for a sixth of a glucose molecule as CH_2O, first because it gives the appearance of a carbon atom to which a molecule of water is attached, and second because it gives the appearance of being a molecule of formaldehyde, and because both appearances represent exploded theories.

Suppose, though, we arrange the CH_2O thus: HCOH. This is still the combination of a carbon atom with an oxygen atom and two hydrogen atoms and therefore represents a sixth of a glucose molecule. It cannot be mistaken for carbon plus water, nor can it be mistaken for formaldehyde, the formula for which is never written in that fashion. Furthermore, it resembles what one would expect a sixth of a glucose molecule to be. (Imagine the formula in Figure 5 to be cut into six pieces by snips through the bonds connecting neighboring carbon atoms, and you will have no less than four HCOH fragments.)

Yet we don't want to give the impression that HCOH is a molecule in its own right. It isn't. It is the hypothetical fragment of a molecule introduced not because it has any real existence at all, but only because it will make our chemical equations easier to write and visualize. Therefore, I will put brackets about it to distinguish it from the real formula for a real molecule. I will write one-sixth of a glucose molecule as [HCOH].

Using the formula for one-sixth of the glucose molecule it becomes possible to write the respiration equation with only one molecule of every other substance involved:

$$[HCOH] + O_2 \xrightarrow{\text{(respiration)}} CO_2 + H_2O + \text{energy}$$

(Equation 6)

Furthermore, the carbon cycle can be written with all its members represented by formulas in the simplest possible way, as in Figure 6.

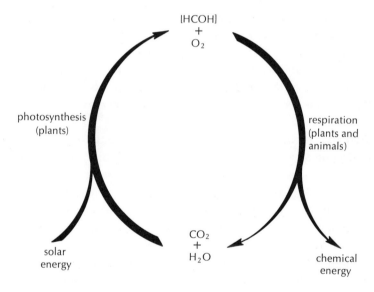

Figure 6. The Carbon Cycle (with Formulas)

Green Leaf

Figure 6 shows the members of the cycle at one end to be glucose and oxygen; and at the other end, carbon dioxide and water. But does that exhaust the list of key members?

Surely not! The carbon cycle does not turn by itself. If it did, it would turn and keep turning in all forms of life—but it does not! It turns and keeps turning in plants; while it does not in animals. In animals, it turns half way, from glucose and oxygen to carbon dioxide and water. It does not make the return trip.

Presumably there is something in plants that is not present in animals and that makes the return trip possible. And surely that "something" is another key member of the cycle.

It is possible to reason out something about the properties of this additional key member of the cycle. It makes photosynthesis possible and the basic fact about photosynthesis is that solar energy is utilized. The substance we are looking for must therefore absorb light.

How does that help us? If a substance does not absorb much light but reflects it generally, it appears white. If it absorbs light generally and efficiently, it appears black. Very many substances that absorb light, however, do not do so generally. They absorb some portions and reflect the rest. The various portions of light seem to our eyes different in color. If a substance absorbs some colors and reflects others, it appears to our eyes to be itself that color which it reflects.

The substance which sparks photosynthesis must absorb light so it cannot be white. It very likely does not absorb all portions of light, so it is very likely colored. If there is a photosynthesizing substance in plants that is not in animals, then it is possible that plants have some color that animals do not have.

Before going further, it is only fair to point out that it is possible for a substance to be colored as a result of partial absorption of light without its having anything to do with photosynthesis. Human blood contains a substance that gives it a red color, but that has nothing to do with its function. Indeed, within the blood vessels, light does not strike the colored substance to any significant degree so that any light-absorbing properties it may have is completely irrelevant to its function. Furthermore, colors can match for reasons that have nothing to do with either chemical structure or function. There are flowers that seem as red as blood, but the redness in the petal and in blood are caused by completely different substances with properties and functions that show no similarity.

With that warning in mind, we can still ask ourselves if there is an overall difference between plant color and animal color that might conceivably have something to do with photosynthesis. And, certainly, there is a very good candidate.

Virtually all plants are green, or have important green parts, whereas no animals are green. (There are green pigments in the feathers of some birds, but there is absolutely no relation between this and the greenness of plants. Green feathers can be ignored.)

It is not difficult to determine that only those portions of a plant that are green can photosynthesize. Non-green portions—flowers, roots, woody regions—do not photosynthesize. There are organisms which seem to be plants by every criterion but which are not green—mushrooms are the best-known example—and they do not photosynthesize.

It seems almost certain, then, without going any further, that some substance that lends plants their green color must be a vital member of the carbon cycle.

In 1817, two French chemists, Pierre Joseph Pelletier and Joseph Bienaimé Caventou, isolated the green substance and named it "chlorophyll" from Greek words meaning "green leaf."

There was no denying its importance to plants, to man, to life generally, but there was also no denying the difficulties of working with it. At the time of its discovery, chemists had no way of dealing with the molecular details of any but the very simplest organic compounds. It took them the remainder of the nineteenth century to develop the tools to the point where they could tackle something as complicated as chlorophyll turned out to be.

The first major attack launched upon it came in 1906 and the chemist involved was the German worker Richard Willstätter. He was the first to prepare chlorophyll in reasonably pure form and he made a number of important discoveries in connection with it.

He found, to begin with, that it was not a single compound but a pair of closely related ones, which differed slightly in their manner of light absorption. He called the pair "chlorophyll *a*" and "chlorophyll *b*." The former was the more common, making up about three-fourths of the mixture.

He also studied the different types of elements found in the chlorophyll molecule. Carbon, hydrogen, oxygen and nitrogen were present, and that was to be expected. These four were present in virtually every substance of complicated structure found in living tissue. In addition, however, there were also magnesium atoms. This was a surprise. Chlorophyll was the first compound of living tissue found to contain that element.

The next step would be to determine how the various atoms of these five varieties were arranged within the chlorophyll molecule, but this was a most formidable problem. From the knowledge we have gained since Willstätter's time, we know that the chlorophyll *a* molecule contains no less than 137 atoms, and chlorophyll *b* 136. The empirical formula of these compounds (with "Mg" the chemical symbol of magnesium) is now known to be $C_{55}H_{72}N_4O_5Mg$ for chlorophyll *a* and $C_{55}H_{70}N_4O_6Mg$ for chlorophyll *b*.

The number of possible arrangements for this number and variety of atoms is enormous and in Willstätter's time there was simply no hope of getting anywhere by working with the intact molecule. The common chemical practice in such cases was to shiver the molecules to pieces by some method or other, then work out the structure of the broken fragments. With luck, it would then be possible to reason out how these fragments might fit together to form the original structure and check the reasoning by appropriate experiments.

Willstätter did treat chlorophyll in such a way as to cause it to break into fragments. The most important piece of information he picked up in this fashion was that the molecular structure of many of those fragments seemed to include what is called a "pyrrole ring." Such a ring is made up of four carbon atoms and a nitrogen atom arranged in a pentagon. The simplest compound containing this ring is pyrrole itself, which is shown in Figure 7.

It seemed reasonable to suppose, then, that whatever the structure of chlorophyll might be, one or more pyrrole rings would be found included in it.

It was at this point that Willstätter left the investigation. For

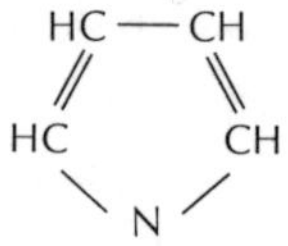

$$HC \overset{\diagup\diagup}{} CH$$

pyrrole (C_4H_4N)

Figure 7. Pyrrole

what he had done, though, and for his work on other colored substances in plants, he received the Nobel Prize for chemistry in 1915.

The Ring of Rings

The torch was taken up by another German chemist, Hans Fischer. His interest focussed at first on the red coloring matter of blood. This color was caused by the presence, in the red corpuscles of blood, of a protein called "hemoglobin." This protein was easily separated into two unequal parts, "heme" (from a Greek word meaning "blood") and "globin."

It is the globin that is the protein proper. Heme is not a protein but is, rather, a relatively small non-protein structure attached to the protein molecule. Proteins, however, are giant molecules and heme can be "relatively small" in comparison yet still be large.

The heme molecule was, in fact, about the size and complexity of the chlorophyll molecule and even had a metallic atom associated with itself, as chlorophyll had. Whereas the chlorophyll molecule contained a magnesium atom, heme possessed an iron atom.

When Fischer began to break down the heme molecule, the similarity to chlorophyll became even more pronounced. As was the case with Willstätter and chlorophyll, Fischer found pyrrole rings in the structure of the fragments. Fischer went further, however. He carried on his investigation until he had convinced himself that the structure of the heme molecule consisted of four pyrrole rings linked together in a circle through bridges made up of single carbon atoms.

Compounds containing such a ring of rings are called "porphyrins" from a Greek word meaning "purple" because many of the compounds are red-purple in color. The simplest porphyrin, one with a molecule made up of the ring of rings with no embellishments at all, is called "porphin" and that is shown in Figure 8.

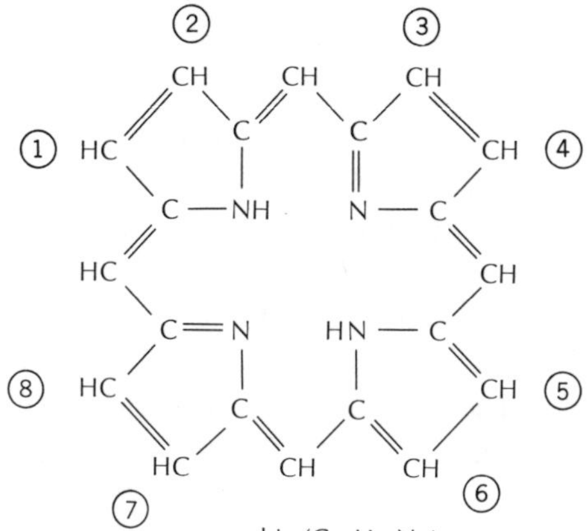

porphin ($C_{20}H_{14}N_4$)

Figure 8. The Porphyrin Ring

Porphin itself does not exist in living tissue. Hans Fischer put it together from simpler structures in 1935 and only then could it be studied directly. The porphyrins found in living tissue have the porphin structure as the core but added to it are small groups of carbon atoms ("side-chains") at the exposed corners of the pyrrole rings, numbered 1 to 8 in Figure 8.

Fischer's decision that heme was a porphyrin in nature was fine as far as it went, but the question still remained: Which derivative? What were the different side-chains in heme, and in which particular position was each side-chain?

To determine that, Fischer closely examined the different pyrroles he had obtained from the smashed heme molecule to see what side-chains were attached to them. The pyrrole ring, smaller than the porphyrin ring, yielded its secrets more readily.

He decided that distributed among the eight positions on the porphyrin ring were four side-chains of one carbon each, two of two carbons each and three of three carbons each. There were fifteen different ways, however, in which these side-chains could be arranged about the porphyrin ring and it was necessary to know which arrangement was the one that occurred in heme.

To answer that question, Fischer decided to put together a sample of each possible arrangement, and for that purpose he divided his students into fifteen groups and had each group tackle the synthesis of a different arrangement. As each one was formed he tested its properties to see how it compared to those of the porphyrin obtained from heme itself.

It turned out that the porphyrin he was after had the one-carbon side-chains in positions 1, 3, 5, and 8; the two carbon side-chains in positions 2 and 4; and the three-carbon side-chains in positions 6 and 7. An iron atom in the center of such a porphyrin gave him heme. (The iron atom has, as its chemical symbol, "Fe," from the Latin word for that metal, "ferrum." Iron, as it occurs in heme, is not quite an ordinary atom, however. It bears a double charge of positive electricity for reasons that need not concern us and it can be symbolized as Fe^{++}.) The formula of heme is presented in Figure 9.

Fischer completed his elucidation of the structure of the heme molecule in 1930 and that very year, without delay, he was awarded the Nobel Prize for chemistry.

The reason for going into these details on heme structure are two-fold. First, it has a direct bearing on the structure of chlorophyll and second, it plays an important role in the carbon cycle.

Heme is best known to us as a constituent of hemoglobin, which is the oxygen-carrying compound in blood. As blood passes through the thin-walled vessels that hug the membranes of the lung, oxygen molecules drift across thin membranes and attach themselves loosely to the iron atoms of the heme molecule.

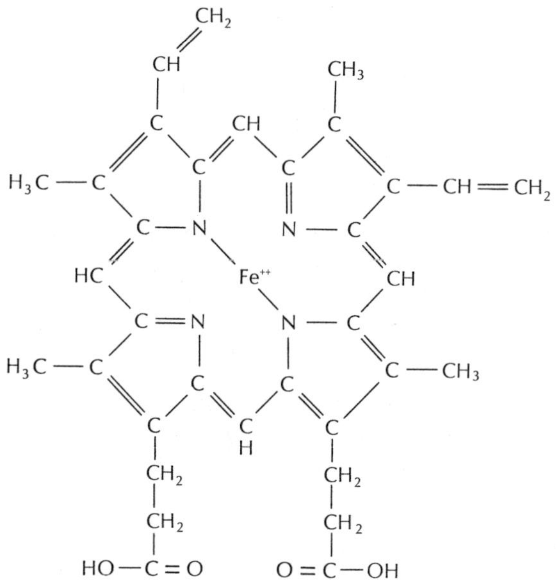

heme ($C_{34}H_{32}O_4N_4Fe$)

Figure 9. Heme

The oxygen-carrying hemoglobin ("oxyhemoglobin") is carried by the blood to the body generally, where the oxygen is given up to the tissues.* Yet this is not the key service rendered by heme to life generally. Hemoglobin is characteristic of vertebrates, but many invertebrate animals use other types of compounds to transport oxygen, or, if they are small enough, can dispense with special transport mechanisms altogether.

Heme is, however, attached to other proteins also. In particular, it is to be found in a family of proteins called "cytochromes" which handle the oxygen molecules once they pass from the blood into the tissues. These cytochromes are indispensable to energy production via the carbon cycle. All plants and animals, large and small, whether they have hemoglobin or not, possess the cytochromes.

* For more detail, see my book *The Living River* (New York: Abelard-Schuman, 1960).

Adding a Tail

Once having worked out the structure of heme, Fischer went on to tackle that of chlorophyll which, he was confident, must be quite similar.

The similarity proved to be close indeed in some respects. The porphyrin ring formed the core of the chlorophyll molecule just as it formed the core of the heme molecule. Side-chains 1, 3, 5, and 8 were one-carbon groups in chlorophyll as in heme, side-chains 2 and 4 were two-carbon groups, and side-chains 6 and 7 were, after a fashion, three-carbon groups.

There were differences, though. There is, of course, a magnesium atom carrying a double positive charge (Mg^{++}) in place of the iron in heme. The side-chain in position 4 of chlorophyll, while two carbons in length, lacks the double bond present in the corresponding position in heme. In one pyrrole ring, one of the double bonds present in heme is missing in chlorophyll.

It is in the three-carbon side-chains that the most complicated differences lie. In heme, these side-chains hang free and uncomplicated. This is not so in chlorophyll. The one in position 6 whips about to join the one-carbon bridge nearby, forming an additional small ring (a fifth). Some additional atoms are added also.

The three-carbon side-chain in position 7 is attached to a long 20-carbon chain called the "phytyl group" and this is the most noticeable difference of all. You can see all this quite clearly in the formula of chlorophyll a, which is given in Figure 10 and which you should compare with the formula of heme in Figure 9. You will see that chlorophyll is very much like heme with an added tail.

Chlorophyll b differs from chlorophyll a only in the side-chain in position 3. In chlorophyll a the one-carbon side-chain is -CH₃ while in chlorophyll b it is -CHO instead. In consequence, chlorophyll b has one oxygen atom more than chlorophyll a and two hydrogen atoms less.

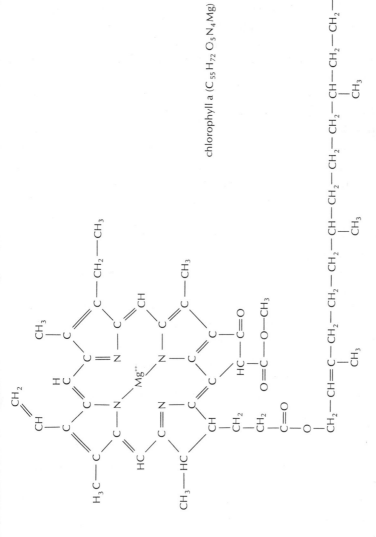

Figure 10. Chlorophyll

Chlorophyll is not the only colored substance found in photo-synthesizing tissues. They all contain other kinds as well. Of these, the most important are those grouped under the heading of "carotenoids." These tend to be red, orange or yellow in color. (The color of the carrot, for instance, is due to a carotenoid and it is from the carrot that this class of pigment received its name.)

The carotene molecules are made up of 40-carbon chains. The 20-carbon phytyl chain attached to the chlorophyll molecule is, in effect, half a carotenoid molecule. A part (but not all) of the function of the carotenoids in plant tissue is to serve as the source of the phytyl group.

The determination of the structure of heme and chlorophyll did not at once make entirely clear the manner in which these important compounds functioned. That would have been too much to expect, for we live in a subtle universe that doesn't yield its secrets easily to even the most determined and ingenious as-saults. (How dull it would be for all of us if it did!)

Nevertheless, as we shall see, increasing knowledge about the carbon cycle is forcing the complicated ring of rings that makes up the molecules of heme and chlorophyll to have more and more meaning. Its complications are beginning to "make sense."

Of course, in pursuing the meaning of the complicated atomic arrangements of these key members of the carbon cycle, it would help if we knew we were truly working with the correct arrange-ments. Chemists consider the best proof of structure of any par-ticular molecule to be the synthesis of that structure from scratch and a demonstration that the structure so synthesized does indeed have all the properties of the substance it is supposed to represent.

Hans Fischer had synthesized heme, and that was all right. The correctness of heme shed additional plausibility on the care-fully worked out structure of the chlorophyll molecule, but the final proof by synthesis eluded all efforts for years. It was not until 1960 that the American chemist Robert Burns Woodward managed to synthesize chlorophyll and to show that its accepted formula was indeed correct. For this (and for other important and complicated syntheses) he received the Nobel Prize for chem-istry in 1965.

Within the Cell

If we extract chlorophyll from plant tissues in pure form and supply it, in the test tube, with carbon dioxide, water, and sunlight, we will find that photosynthesis will *not* take place. Even if we throw in the carotenes and any other pure substances we find in plant cells, it will not help.

Apparently, within plant tissue, chlorophyll is part of an intricate and well-organized mechanism that acts as a smoothly-working whole to carry through a photosynthetic process that includes many steps. Chlorophyll makes the key step possible and without it nothing can happen, but the key step, by itself, is not enough.

(To draw an analogy from the more familiar world of the automobile—the ignition key sets in motion a whole series of events in the complicated automotive mechanism and starts you moving over the road at a rapid rate of speed. However, if all you have is an ignition key and nothing else, it won't get you moving even if you sit down on the road and pile a heap of loose automobile parts all about yourself.)

If we wish to study the organization of an animal or plant, we find the smallest unit which can conveniently act as a self-contained whole is the "cell." An average cell is perhaps 1/750 of an inch in diameter, so it is not visible to the naked eye and can be studied only under a microscope. Each cell is marked off from the outside world (and from other cells) by a thin membrane of well-organized structure including molecules of both proteins and of fatty substances.

An adult human being is made up of some fifty trillion (50,-000,000,000,000) cells. Each is so specialized that it depends on the other cells of the body to perform functions it cannot perform by itself, so that the individual human cell cannot survive in isolation.

Yet that does not suffice to downgrade the importance of the individual cell. The human being (and all other organisms built of many cells) begins life as a single, independently-existing cell. Furthermore, there are some tiny forms of life that are made up of single cells. There are one-celled animals ("protozoa") and one-celled plants ("algae"). The bacteria, which are not properly either animals or plants, are also single-celled. (There are viruses, too, which are less than cells, but these will not concern us in this book.)

Within the cell, there is further specialization. That is, there are present "organelles" each of which performs some one special function. These organelles are not easy to see. Ordinary cells, viewed under an ordinary microscope, in the bright light necessary to make small objects visible after magnification, are virtually transparent, and little detail can be seen within.

Biologists therefore subjected the cells to solutions of various dyes in the hope that different parts of the cell—specialized for different purposes and therefore containing different substances—might react in different manner to the dye. Some parts of the cell might absorb the dye while other parts might not. Thus, detail within the cell might become visible in color.

In this way, for instance, the controlling organelles of the cell and of life were discovered. These were to be found in the "nucleus," a small body located more or less in the center of each cell, and separated from the rest of the cell by a thin membrane. Within that nucleus, thread-like organelles contain the substances involved in cell division and in heredity. Because these organelles were detected by their ability to absorb a red dye, they were called "chromosomes" ("colored bodies") even though they are colorless in actuality.

In 1898, a German biologist, C. Benda, studied cells by means of the application of a dye system of his own devising. He found that this brought out tiny granules outside the nucleus, in that portion of the cell called the "cytoplasm." He called these granules "mitochondria." (The singular form is "mitochondrion.")

As the decades passed, it was found that the cytoplasm of all cells capable of respiration, contained these mitochondria and that it was the mitochondria that contained the machinery for the respiratory half of the carbon cycle. They contained all that was necessary for the handling of molecular oxygen, for the oxidation of glucose—and, indeed, for the oxidation of carbohydrates, fat, and protein generally. They contained, in particular, the various molecules of the cytochrome family.

The average mitochondrion is shaped like a very tiny football, about 1/10,000 of an inch long and 1/25,000 of an inch thick. An average cell might contain anywhere from several hundred to a thousand mitochondria. Very large cells may contain a couple of hundred thousand, while certain bacteria which make no use of molecular oxygen contain none.

The tiny mitochondrion is so small that it can be made out as a mere, featureless granule under an ordinary microscope. In the the 1930's physicists developed the "electron microscope," a device that is capable of magnifications a hundred times as great as that made possible by an ordinary microscope.

After World War II, the electron microscope was assiduously applied to the study of the internal structure of cells and it was discovered that the tiny mitochondrion had a complex structure of its own, for all its tiny size. The mitochondrion has a double membrane; the outer one smooth and the inner one elaborately wrinkled to present a large surface. The membranes consist of protein molecules that give it a continuous structure, and these are coated with a layer of fat-like molecules that insulate the proteins and prevent them from building up in three dimensions, keeping them a flat layer one molecule in thickness.

Along the inner surface of the mitochondrion, and probably forming an integral portion of that surface, are several thousand tiny structures called "elementary particles." It is these elementary particles that may represent the actual oxidation machinery.

Included in the machinery are a number of fragile protein molecules of specific structure. The many chemical reactions making up the respiratory half of the carbon cycle are each under control of a particular one of these proteins. Such a reaction-controlling protein is called an "enzyme," and where an enzyme is not present, the reaction it controls can take place only very slowly.

It is the careful organization of the proper enzymes in the proper order that makes a complex set of reactions move smoothly and efficiently.

Along with the enzymes are relatively small non-protein molecules that can attach themselves loosely to one or another of several enzymes and that act as carriers for atomic groups cut loose from larger molecules by the enzyme-controlled reaction. Those small molecules are called "coenzymes" since they cooperate with enzymes. Present also are electrically charged metal atoms which keep enzymes active and which are therefore called "activators." The individual mitochondrion contains all necessary items for respiration—enzymes, coenzymes and activators.

We may imagine a glucose molecule, for instance, moving through a mitochondrion, and being efficiently altered in structure in one fashion, then another, then another, as one enzyme (with such coenzymes and activators as may be necessary) after another is brought into place. Oxygen molecules entering at another point are also handled in an appropriate manner. After a very short interval of time, what was glucose and oxygen has become carbon dioxide and water, and the energy produced is made available to the cell generally. The mitochondrion, in short, is a kind of chemical assembly line.

And what about an organelle to handle the photosynthetic half of the carbon cycle. This would have to contain chlorophyll and would, therefore, be green. Naturally, if an organelle is already colored, it does not have to be dyed. It can be seen directly. As soon, then, as the ordinary microscope had been refined to the point where tiny bodies within the cell could be seen, at least as dots, it became possible to tell whether chlorophyll was spread evenly throughout the cell or was concentrated within organelles.

The latter was the case and, in 1883, Julius Sachs demonstrated that. Eventually, these chlorophyll-containing organelles were named "chloroplasts."

Chloroplasts are, generally, considerably larger than mitochondria. Some one-celled plants possess only one large chloroplast per cell. Most plant cells, however, contain many smaller chloroplasts. Even so, the average chloroplast is two to three times as long and as thick as a mitochondrion.

The structure of the chloroplast seems to be even more complex than that of the mitochondrion. The interior of the chloroplast is made up of many thin membranes stretching across from wall to wall. These are the "lamellae." In most types of chloroplasts, these lamellae thicken and darken in places to make dark condensations called "grana." The chlorophyll molecules are to be found within the grana.

If the lamellae within the grana are studied under the electron microscope, they, in turn, seem to be made up of tiny units, just barely visible, that look like the neatly laid tiles of a bathroom floor. Each of these objects may be a photosynthesizing unit containing 250 to 300 chlorophyll molecules.

The chloroplasts are more difficult to handle than mitochondria are. When cells are broken up, mitochondria can be isolated, intact, with relative ease, and can, after careful isolation, continue to perform their function. Chloroplasts are apparently more fragile. In 1937, chloroplasts were isolated from broken cells but they were not sufficiently intact to carry through photosynthesis. (They did, however, demonstrate the "Hill reaction" which I will discuss in its appropriate place later in the book.)

It was not until 1954, that Daniel I. Arnon, working with disrupted spinach leaf cells, was able to obtain chloroplasts completely intact and able to carry through the complete photosynthetic reaction.

The chloroplast—thus shown finally to be a self-contained photosynthetic unit—contains the complete assembly-line for the purpose within itself. It contains not only chlorophyll and carotenoids, but a full complement of enzymes, coenzymes and activators as well, all properly and intricately arranged. It even contains cytochromes, ordinarily associated with respiration, but present in the chloroplast for, as we shall see, good and sufficient reason. (In view of all this, it is no wonder that chlorophyll by itself cannot carry through photosynthesis.)

The chloroplast is less amenable than the mitochondrion to

manipulation from outside. The respiration reactions within mitochondria could be hastened or slowed by the addition of various compounds to respiring cells. In this way, it was possible to make deductions as to what was going on within the mitochondrion.

This technique did not work with the apparently better-insulated chloroplast. As a result, biochemists worked out the chemical details of respiration before they could manage to do the same for photosynthesis.

We see from all this, then, that in discussing the respiratory and photosynthetic halves of the carbon cycle, we have, until now, been unnecessarily broad in speaking of "plants" and "animals." We might better narrow the focus by concentration on those organelles that actually carry through these halves, in whatever cell or organism they might exist. This is done in Figure 11.

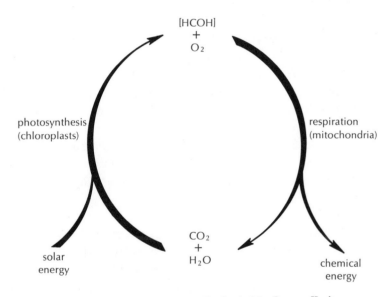

Figure 11. The Carbon Cycle (with Organelles)

3

The Product of the Cycle

Kilocalories per Mole

We have been gradually sharpening the various portions of the carbon cycle. For food and air, we have substituted glucose and oxygen and made use of the chemical formulas. We have pinned down the major source of plant nutrition as carbon dioxide and water and used the formulas there, too. We have narrowed the accomplishment of respiration and photosynthesis from entire organisms down to mitochondria and chloroplasts, respectively.

One thing only remains unchanged from the very beginning of our representation of the carbon cycle in Figure 1 to the most recent version in Figure 11—energy. We are still speaking of chemical energy as the product of respiration and of solar energy as the factor pushing along photosynthesis. Can we not sharpen that as well? Let us at least try.

Energy is a large subject, the central concern of the science of physics and representing an all-important background to the sciences of chemistry and biology.* It might even be considered a looming side-issue in the social sciences, since much of human history, economics and sociology is based on the nature and the comparative availability, to various segments of Earth's population, of the energy sources of the world.

For our purposes in this book, we can accept the fact that the most characteristic form of energy is heat, and, further, that any-

* For considerable detail on the subject, see my book *Life and Energy* (New York: Doubleday, 1961).

thing else is a form of energy if it can be converted completely
into heat.

In measuring the amount of energy present in any system, then,
it would be natural to convert that energy into heat first and measure that. The easiest way to measure the quantity of heat evolved
in some system is to encase the entire system within a container
suspended in a sizable quantity of water at known temperature
—water that is insulated so that it will not gain heat from the
outside or lose heat to it.

As heat is produced within the container, it will flow out into
the water, which will not lose it (or will lose very little) and will
gain no heat (or very little) from other sources. The temperature
of the water will rise. Since the temperature of a given quantity
of water rises by a known amount for some given input of energy,
we can measure heat production from temperature rise—and to
measure temperature rise is quite simple.

Suppose, for instance, we imagine heat pouring into a container
of water at 14.5° C. (58.1° F.) and we concentrate our attention
on 1 gram of that water.*

If the temperature of the water generally rises 1 Celsius degree
to 15.5° C. (59.9° F.) then the particular gram of water we have
been keeping our eye on gains an amount of heat that is called
"1 calorie."

Naturally, every single gram of that water has absorbed 1 calorie of heat as the temperature goes up from 14.5° C. to 15.5° C.
If there are a thousand grams of water altogether, then that quantity of water absorbs 1000 calories of heat as its temperature goes
up that 1 Celsius degree. We can define 1000 calories as a
"kilocalorie."

When we burn any substance, heat and light are given off. We
have agreed that heat is energy to begin with. Light is also a form

---

* C. stands for the Celsius scale, used by scientists all over the world. F.
is the Fahrenheit scale used for everyday purposes in the United States
and Great Britain. A gram is a unit of mass (usually, but incorrectly,
called "weight" by most people) in the metric system, which is official in
almost every nation of the world except for the United States and Great
Britain. A gram is a small unit of mass for it takes 28.35 grams to
equal 1 avoirdupois ounce.

of energy for when absorbed by any opaque substance it turns completely into heat. Now, then, what is the energy given off by burning coal in kilocalories?

We can't measure the energy given off by a lump of coal that is burning in a fireplace. The heat and light both escape. If, however, we burn a small piece of coal in an enclosed vessel which has been supplied with sufficient oxygen for the purpose and we enclose that vessel in a jacket of water at known temperature, the situation is different. From the rise in temperature of the water, we can tell that 1 gram of coal will give off a little over $7\frac{1}{2}$ kilocalories of energy.

Naturally, the quantity of energy given off by a burning substance depends upon the total amount of substance that undergoes the burning. Chemists might agree to use 1 gram of any substance as the standard, but they have chosen not to. It is more convenient, from the standpoint of chemical calculations, to use some fixed number of molecules as the standard. They have chosen (for good and sufficient reasons that don't concern our subject in this book) to use the number of carbon atoms in 12 grams of carbon as their standard. This number is naturally an enormous one. It is equal to 602,600,000,000,000,000,000,000. This number of atoms (or molecules) of any substance is called a "mole."

A mole of water has a mass of 18 grams, and a mole of glucose has a mass of 180 grams. The mole of glucose has ten times the mass of the mole of water because the individual molecule of glucose has ten times the mass of the individual molecule of water. The use of the mole, therefore, allows for differences in mass among molecules.

Suppose then we combine glucose and oxygen in a closed vessel surrounded by insulated water at known temperature. (Such a set-up is known as a "calorimeter" from Latin words meaning "heat-measure.") Having measured the heat evolved from the combination with oxygen of a known amount of glucose, we can easily calculate how much heat would be evolved if a mole of glucose had been completely oxidized. That quantity, it turns out, would be 673.0 kilocalories.

We can express this succinctly by saying: The heat of combustion of glucose is 673.0 kilocalories per mole, or, abbreviating, 673.0 kcal/mole.

That, however, is the situation one finds when glucose is well-mixed with oxygen and the reaction is allowed to take place with explosive rapidity. This is not, however, what happens in the body. In living tissue, glucose is never mixed with pure oxygen; it does not react with explosive rapidity. Instead, it is slowly and gradually changed, through a large number of steps, into carbon dioxide and water.

This is different altogether and it is tempting to suspect that living tissue makes shrewd and cunning use of glucose; treats it in such a way as to extract unusual quantities of energy from it.

However, this is not so.

In the mid-nineteenth century, physicists worked out what is called "the law of conservation of energy." From large numbers of observations, they concluded that although energy could be shifted from place to place and changed from one form into another, it could be neither created from nothing nor destroyed into nothing. No one man can be truly credited with enunciating this law, but the first clear and convincing statement came in 1847 from the German physiologist Hermann von Helmholtz.

The law of conservation of energy meant that the energy produced by the oxidation of glucose to carbon dioxide and water would have to be the same no matter what route it followed or under what auspices it took place—in a metal container or in the human body.

It's all very well to say such things on the basis of theory, but can we be sure? Suppose the theory is wrong. Wouldn't it be better actually to measure the energy produced by glucose oxidation in living tissue?

Of course, it would. Lavoisier himself tried to do so, half a century before the law of conservation of energy was thoroughly understood. His methods were too primitive to prove much, but in 1849, only two years after Helmholtz's announcement, a French chemist, Henri Victor Regnault, devised a box into which an animal could be placed, into which measured amounts of oxygen could be led and from which the carbon dioxide produced by the animal could be collected and weighed.

By the end of the century boxes were made large enough to hold a man, and the methods of measurement were made quite precise. The climax was reached in the 1880's and 1890's through the meticulous work of the German physiologist Max Rubner. His calorimetric measurements of living organisms showed beyond any doubt that the law of conservation of energy held in living tissue as well as in the non-living universe.

The Open Part

The existence of the law of conservation of energy and its strict application to living organisms raises a question which I have so far carefully avoided mentioning.

The carbon cycle, which I have presented several times so far in this book, in ever-sharpening detail, is indeed closed with respect to matter. That is, as the cycle goes round and round, glucose, oxygen, carbon dioxide and water are formed and consumed, formed and consumed, over and over again. In the long run, therefore, they are neither formed nor consumed but remain in constant quantity.

As far as the mitochondria and the chloroplasts are concerned, they, too, remain unchanged in the course of the cycle.

But (and it is a large "but") the same does not appear to be true of energy, as I have pictured matters so far. Energy is the open part of the cycle. Chemical energy is produced by the cycle, but the diagrams simply show the arrow pointing at nothing. Does the energy simply vanish?

Similarly, solar energy comes into the cycle. It is from the Sun, obviously, but how does the Sun produce it? From nowhere?

Certainly, if we considered only the law of conservation of energy, we would have to conclude that the chemical energy produced by the cycle does *not* vanish. It may be utilized in the body for a hundred purposes but it is always there, whatever changes of nature and place it might undergo. And, in the end, could it not be pictured as being gathered together to enter the other end of the cycle, the photosynthetic end?

To be sure, it is the energy of sunlight that enters the cycle in actual fact, but that might only be a matter of convenience. After all, solar energy is so easily and continuously available. But might not plants adapt themselves in such a fashion, someday, as to make themselves independent of sunlight and close the carbon cycle altogether, allowing the energy produced by respiration to enter the cycle again in the photosynthesis portion.

The carbon cycle would then look as shown in Figure 12, and nothing in Figure 12 violates the law of conservation of energy.

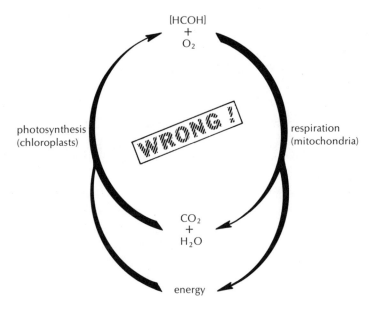

Figure 12. The Carbon Cycle (as Closed to Energy)

Yet the situation as shown in Figure 12 *does not and cannot happen!* This fact is so important that I don't dare allow Figure 12 to remain in this book without warning, lest a casual browser, leafing through these pages, see the diagram without actually reading this section, and think it is so. For that reason, I write WRONG over the cycle.

It is the experience of mankind that although energy does not disappear, it is not always available for use. Water running spontaneously down from a height will turn a water wheel. The water wheel will never spontaneously turn to push the water back up to the height. When a hot object sits in contact with a cool one, the hot object cools off and the cool object warms up until both are at the same temperature. Two objects in contact and at the same temperature will never spontaneously change in such a way that one body grows hot while the other grows cold.

Such examples can be multiplied endlessly. The point is that while energy is neither produced nor destroyed, it seems to flow in one direction *only*. This is called the "second law of thermodynamics."* The "first law" is the conservation of energy.

This one-way motion of energy is easily compared with the one-way motion of matter in the earth's gravitational field. Water flows downward spontaneously, never upward.

Some chemical reactions take place spontaneously (though sometimes very slowly) and such reactions involve a "downward" flow of energy. We can call these "downhill reactions." Others don't ever take place spontaneously (no matter how slowly) because they involve an "upward" flow of energy. They are "uphill reactions."

In the carbon cycle, respiration is a downhill reaction and photosynthesis an uphill reaction. That is why I have drawn the carbon cycle with the respiration arrow pointing downward and the photosynthesis arrow pointing upward.

To explain the one-way motion of energy, physicists have devised a quantity termed "entropy." One way of describing entropy is to suppose that it represents the amount of disorder in the universe.

Disorder is a much more probable situation than order. Very

* Thermodynamics (from Greek words meaning "heat-movement") is the study of the relationship between heat and other forms of energy.

few situations may be described as orderly, but very, very many as disorderly. For instance, there is only one way in which the playing cards in a deck are in exact order (ace of spades, two of spades, three of spades and so on) but many trillions of ways in which they may not be in exact order and therefore in some degree of disorder. For that reason, if you shuffle a deck which is in order to begin with, and it assumes any order at random, that new order is sure to be disorderly.

Physicists have demonstrated to their complete satisfaction that in *any* spontaneous change, there is bound to be some increase in disorder; that is, in entropy. Indeed, if there is any change in which entropy decreases, that change will not take place spontaneously.

Now comes the crucial point. Whenever some spontaneous process produces energy, some of that energy cannot be converted into usable forms. It is there, but it can't be used; it is unavailable. The quantity of unavailable energy is equal to the increase in entropy taking place in the process, multiplied by the absolute temperature.*

What is left over, the part of the energy that *is* available for use, is called "free energy."

Now we can see why the situation as shown in Figure 12 is impossible. To bring carbon dioxide and water back to glucose and oxygen requires an input of the exact amount of energy released in converting glucose and oxygen to carbon and water. That is necessary by the first law of thermodynamics—conservation of energy.

However, of the energy released in converting glucose and oxygen, some is made unavailable through entropy increase. The available energy that is left is insufficient to re-form the glucose and oxygen.

To keep the cycle running, more energy must be continually added to it from the outside. Fortunately, such addition does take place—in the form of the energy of sunlight.

---

* The absolute temperature is counted from "absolute zero" which is 273.1 Celsius degrees below 0° C.

We conclude, then, that the carbon cycle *is* open as far as energy is concerned. The free energy produced by respiration is utilized to run one uphill reaction after another, and at each reaction, some more of it becomes unavailable as entropy is increased until, in the end, there is no free energy left at all. All the energy that was there is still there but it is no longer available. There is no more *free* energy.

The carbon cycle serves to form a continuous stream of *new* free energy to replace the old supply that is used up forever.

Electron-volts per Molecule

Instead of talking about the heat of combustion, then, let us consider the amount of free energy produced in the conversion of glucose and oxygen to carbon dioxide and energy. To be sure, this quantity varies somewhat with change of condition. (The total energy output would not vary but its division into available and unavailable fractions could.) Chemists, however, set certain conditions as "standard" and calculate what the free energy change would be under those standard conditions. They then have the "standard free energy change" which they symbolize as $\Delta F°$.

For the oxidation of glucose by oxygen to form carbon dioxide and water, the standard free energy change is —686 kilocalories per mole of glucose.

The standard free energy change is negative, for the system loses free energy. That is, the mixture of glucose and oxygen at the start is richer in free energy than is the mixture of carbon dioxide and water at the end. In passing from the original state to the final state, 686 kilocalories of free energy per mole leave the system and enter the outside world.

We can therefore write the respiration equation for an entire molecule of glucose (see Equation 5 on page 34) with a precise amount of free energy included, rather than merely the vague word "energy." Nor need we include the term "respiration" on the arrow any longer. The standard free energy change would be the same whether the change were part of respiration or not. The equation would now look thus:

$$C_6H_{12}O_6 + 6O_2 - 686 \text{ kcal/mole} \longrightarrow 6CO_2 + 6H_2O$$

(Equation 7)

Whenever a system loses free energy in the process of some change, there is always a gain in entropy. The loss of free energy is as sure a sign that a reaction is spontaneous and "downhill," therefore, as is the gain in entropy. The change in free energy happens to be easier to measure than the change in entropy, so it is the free energy change that is usually used as a guide to the spontaneity of a reaction. The oxidation of glucose involves a loss of free energy and, for that reason alone, can be seen to be spontaneous.

In Equation 7, we are working with whole molecules of glucose. If we wish to switch once more to sixth-molecules of glucose, we must divide every item in the equation by six, including the free energy loss. Thus:

$$[HCOH] + O_2 - 114 \text{ kcal/mole} \longrightarrow CO_2 + H_2O$$

(Equation 8)

But we are still left with an incongruity. We are trying to deal with single molecules of substances, yet we are also dealing with the free energy produced by moles of substance, with each mole equal to nearly a million billion billion molecules.

Is there any convenient way of sticking to single molecules throughout and speaking of the free energy loss in the oxidation of a single sixth-molecule of glucose? There is a way, of course. We need only divide 114 kcal/mole by the number of molecules in a mole. The free energy loss for the oxidation of a sixth-molecule would then turn out to be 0.00000000000000000000002 kilocalories.

This is a way, but not a convenient way. To use so small a fraction would be intolerable.

Usually, however, there are a number of different kinds of units, of widely different sizes, for any particular type of measurement. If one unit is of an inconvenient size, we can use another.

For instance, in ordinary life, Americans measure length in inches, feet, yards, furlongs, or miles. We could, if we wished, measure the distance from home to City Hall in inches, but that would not be convenient and miles are used instead. Conversely, we could, if we wished, measure the length of this page as a certain fraction of a mile, but everyone would surely use inches instead.

What we need then is a unit of energy considerably smaller than the kilocalorie. Physicists frequently use the "erg" as a unit of energy. (The name of the unit is the middle syllable of "energy.") The erg is much smaller than the kilocalorie, for 1 kilocalorie is equal to 41,860,000,000 ergs, but it is still not small enough for molecular-sized pieces of energy.

We can, however, sink down another large step, to a unit of energy first introduced by nuclear physicists who had to deal with the energies involved in handling single particles that were often far smaller in size than even a single atom.

This is the "electron-volt," usually and conveniently abbreviated "ev." A single erg is equal to 625,000,000,000 ev.

If, then, a mole of glucose on combining with oxygen loses 686 kilocalories of free energy, then a single molecule of glucose on combining with oxygen loses 30 electron-volts, and a sixth-molecule of glucose would lose 5 electron-volts. We can now write the respiration equation:

$$[HCOH] + O_2 - 5ev \longrightarrow CO_2 + H_2O$$

(Equation 9)

Equation 9 can be written, with equal validity, when the free energy component is shifted to the right-hand side of the equation. In that case (as in algebraic equations) the sign must shift from minus to plus and the equation becomes:

$$[HCOH] + O_2 \longrightarrow CO_2 + H_2O + 5ev$$

(Equation 10)

In Equation 9 we are saying that the mixture of glucose and oxygen loses free energy in becoming a mixture of carbon dioxide and water. In Equation 10, we are saying when glucose and oxygen combine and become a mixture of carbon dioxide and water the universe outside the system gains free energy.

We can now draw a representation of the carbon cycle with still one more item sharpened. We need no longer speak of "chemical energy"; we can supply a precise quantity (see Figure 13).

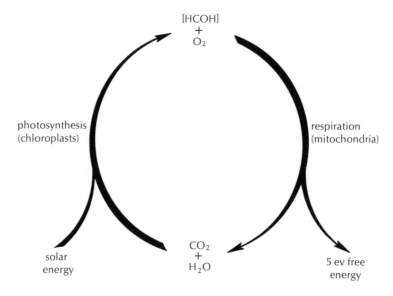

Figure 13. The Carbon Cycle (with Electron-volts)

Coupling the Reactions

The second law of thermodynamics tells us that some reactions are spontaneous and some are not. And it turns out that, from thermodynamic considerations, some of the most important reactions that take place in living tissue are *not* spontaneous and, left to themselves, will never take place.

The key processes within living tissue involve the formation of large and complex molecules (such as proteins and nucleic acids) from small and simple ones. Indeed, the ability to build the large and complex out of the small and simple comes close to being a definition of life in chemical terms.

Yet in general the formation of large molecules from small— of complex molecules from simple—requires an input of free energy. We might imagine the process, in its simplest form, as involving the formation of large molecules by the addition of single atom after single atom to the small starting molecule, and the formation of chemical bond after chemical bond. With each new chemical bond formed, a certain input of free energy is required.

The amount of free energy needed varies somewhat from bond to bond, depending upon the nature of the atoms involved and also upon the particular arrangement already existing in the neighborhood of the bond being formed. (This is similar to the way in which the price of a house varies partly with the nature of the house and partly with the nature of the neighborhood in which it is located.)

For bonds of the types found in protein and nucleic acid molecules, the input of free energy required is from 0.04 to 0.16 ev. We might call the amount 0.1 ev as a nice round-number average.

But the mere fact that free energy is required at all—that the change from simple to complex involves a free energy increase, however small—means that the reaction is not spontaneous. Left to itself, protein and nucleic acid molecules will *not* form from simple substances. Nor can the reaction be made to take place unless the required free energy is supplied.

How can the free energy be supplied? There is no convenient reservoir within the body into which we can dip for pure free energy. (Let us forget sunlight for a moment. It is a special case and I will get back to it in time.) All that one can do, within animal tissues at least, is to "couple" two chemical reactions.

Suppose Reaction 1 involves a decrease in free energy, while Reaction 2 involves an increase. Suppose the decrease involved in Reaction 1 is greater than the increase involved in Reaction 2.

The energy supplied by Reaction 1 will then be sufficient to drive Reaction 2.

Let us suppose, just to pick figures at random, that the decrease in free energy involved in Reaction 1 is 1.0 ev per molecule, and the increase in free energy involved in reaction 2 is 0.8 ev per molecule. If the two reactions take place simultaneously, the net free energy change is $-1.0 + 0.8$ or -0.2 ev per molecule. There is a net decrease in free energy for the two reactions taken together. Although Reaction 2 is not spontaneous and cannot take place *left to itself*, it becomes spontaneous and can take place if it is part of the coupled Reaction 1 and 2.

Let us see what this means in terms of a more familiar mechanical analogy. Imagine that you have weight x resting at one end of a lever, and that you would like to get weight x into a net suspended two feet above the lever. You can wait till the end of time and weight x will not move two feet upward by itself.

Suppose, though, you couple that upward movement of weight x (which is, in itself, not spontaneous) with the downward movement of weight y when this weight is allowed to fall onto the raised end of the lever.

The energy released by weight y as it falls is transferred by the lever to weight x, which is hurled upward. If the energy released by weight y is not as great as that required to move weight x two feet upward, then weight x will move up part way and fall back to the lever. Nothing will have been accomplished.

If the energy released by weight y as it falls is great enough to lift weight x the required two feet, then weight x will drop into the net. The coupled reaction will be a spontaneous one and weight x, which could never move into the net of itself, moves into the net neatly when the motion is part of the coupled reaction.

Within living tissue such coupled reactions result in the formation of complex molecules that would never form of themselves. However, there is nothing in life that can defeat the laws of thermodynamics. The same coupled reactions that are thermodynamically possible in living tissue are thermodynamically possible outside living tissue. Why, then, does life seem to be so much more flexible and versatile than non-life?

The answer is that while thermodynamics tells us that a particular process is spontaneous, it has nothing to say about the speed with which that process will take place. The combination of glucose with oxygen to form carbon dioxide and water is spontaneous, thermodynamically speaking, but that combination ordinarily proceeds unimaginably slowly. Glucose can be allowed to remain in contact with oxygen for prolonged periods without showing perceptible signs of change.

Within the body, however, there exist certain enzymes (see page 55) in whose presence such spontaneous changes can be greatly hastened. How this is done is too complicated a matter to be gone into here, but we might compare the enzymes to the wax on a wooden incline. The presence of the wax will not make it possible for a brick to slide *up* an incline. That is not a spontaneous change and the wax will not alter that. However, a brick will slide *down* the incline much more quickly because of the presence of the wax.

Living tissue contains thousands of enzymes, each of which hastens some one particular reaction. By controlling the kinds of enzymes present and the concentration of each, an unimaginably complex network of coupled reactions takes place within tissue and it is this enzyme-ordered network of reactions that makes up "life."

The next question is this: If we are going to use coupled reactions to bring about uphill changes, how efficient can we make them?

Perfect economy is impossible, of course. The coupled change, by the mere fact that it is spontaneous, will be bound to exhibit an overall increase in entropy. The amount of unavailable energy will increase and this can't be helped.

However, allowing for the entropy change, can we arrange maximum economy otherwise?

Let us return to our mechanical analogy. Consider once again that we are dropping weight y in order to hurl weight x up into the net. No matter what we do we cannot convert all the energy released by weight y into the useful task of lifting weight x into the net. Some of the energy released is bound to be used up in overcoming air resistance to the fall of weight y and the rise of weight x; some is also used up in overcoming the friction involved in the lever motion. Such unavoidable losses through air resistance and friction represent increases in the entropy of the system.

Still, we would find it reasonable to hope that the energy released by the falling weight y would be just sufficient after losses through friction and air resistance to bring weight x exactly up to the net. Suppose instead that the energy released by weight y was sufficient to hurl weight x six feet upward, after which it fell back into the net.

Weight x would still end up in the net and the extra energy that had been sufficient to lift it four feet higher than the shelf would have been simply wasted; it would have accomplished nothing.

If we had an endless number of weights from which to choose our weight y, and if we could drop weight y from any height, then we would choose weight y to be of such a mass and to drop from such a height as to just lift weight x to the net. By careful adjustment, in other words, we would increase our efficiency to very close to the maximum possible.

But suppose we only had two weights to choose from and only one height from which to drop the one we chose. Suppose that one weight released insufficient energy to do the job, while the other weight released three times too much. Which would we choose?

Clearly, between not doing a job at all, and doing it wastefully, we'd have to settle for the waste, provided the job *had* to be done.

With that in mind, let's ask ourselves what "weights" are available to do the body's job. The important uphill reactions in living tissue include the formation of chemical bonds at the average input of 0.1 ev per bond. What is available for coupling in order to make it possible to form these bonds?

The first thought that would occur to us, perhaps, is the combination of glucose and oxygen. Certainly that involves a large decrease in free energy; a decrease that is amply capable of driving the uphill formation of proteins and nucleic acids.

Indeed, the supply of free energy is too ample. The combination of a single molecule of glucose with six oxygen molecules liberates some 30 ev. That is sufficient free energy to form 300 bonds.

But will it form 300 bonds? Can we imagine a glob of energy formed all at once from the conversion of a molecule of glucose to carbon dioxide and water, a glob carefully retained while 300 bonds are formed one after the other at the expense of that energy?

Actually, this is not at all likely. Free energy made available by a chemical reaction must be used at once and, in general, we can expect such liberated free energy to bring about one simple change, say the formation of one bond. Yet can we accept as an alternative the liberation of 30 ev of energy for the sake of the formation of one chemical bond requiring an input of 0.1 ev? That would mean that 99.7 per cent of the energy produced by the glucose molecule would be wasted.

Let's try another analogy. Suppose we were asked to go to the store to buy a carton of cigarettes and were given a five hundred dollar bill for the purpose. The storekeeper would be most unlikely to have change so that we would be faced with the alternative of buying several hundred cartons to use up the money; or of buying the one carton we want and saying, "Keep the change."

Both alternatives are foolish. What we would do would be to go to the bank and change the five hundred dollar bill into small denominations. We could then use one of the small bills to make our purchase and save the rest for other jobs.

So it is with the glucose molecule, which represents a large-denomination bill, if we think of it as combining with oxygen to form carbon dioxide and water in one large step. Rather, why not consider glucose as breaking down by a process involving many stages, forming a series of compounds with a stepwise free energy decrease in comparatively small chunks. It is these individual small free energy decreases (corresponding to the small-denomination bills in our analogy) that are coupled with bond-formation, and with the uphill formation of proteins and nucleic acids.

Breakdown without Oxygen

It was not until the twentieth century, however, that insight into the details of glucose breakdown was gained. In 1918, for instance, the German physiologist Otto Meyerhof was able to show that glucose underwent a partial breakdown in muscle, a breakdown which did not involve oxygen at all. This partial breakdown is referred to as "anaerobic glycolysis" from Greek words meaning "sugar breakdown without air."

For his work on the biochemical details of anaerobic glycolysis, Meyerhof was awarded a share of the 1922 Nobel Prize for physiology and medicine.

Let us describe some of these details, to begin with, in rather broad fashion. When muscle goes into rapid action, its stores of glycogen break down to yield glucose which is, in turn, rapidly consumed. A substance called "lactic acid" appears in the muscle and accumulates.

The empirical formula of lactic acid is $C_3H_6O_3$, which, as far as the number of atoms is concerned, seems to be just half a glucose molecule. This makes it easy to write a balanced equation for the overall change in anaerobic glycolysis, which is the breakdown of glucose to lactic acid:

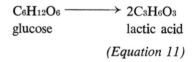

$$C_6H_{12}O_6 \longrightarrow 2C_3H_6O_3$$
glucose   lactic acid

(Equation 11)

Don't think, however, that because the formula of lactic acid, when written simply as the number of various atoms, looks like half a glucose molecule, a lactic acid molecule is indeed half a glucose molecule. It isn't. The arrangement of the atoms in the three-carbon molecule of lactic acid is distinctly different from the arrangement in any three-carbon portion of the glucose molecule, and the properties of lactic acid are correspondingly different from those of glucose. As one quick example, glucose tastes sweet and lactic acid tastes sour.

In general, the breakdown of a large molecule to two or more smaller molecules liberates energy, though, often, not much. In this case about 2.25 ev is made available as free energy for each glucose molecule split to lactic acid. This is equal to 0.37 ev for each sixth-glucose.

To write an equation showing this at the sixth-glucose level, we must have a sixth of a glucose molecule converted into a third of a lactic acid molecule. (We can call the latter a "third-lactic.") The same reasoning that led us to represent the sixth-glucose as [HCOH] (see page 41) would lead us to represent a third-lactic by the same formula. To distinguish them, let's represent a third-lactic as $[HCOH]_L$.

There is, I admit, a certain artificiality in using symbols for molecular fragments that don't exist in reality, but I submit to it because it helps us concentrate on a single carbon atom. With this in mind, and placing the energy change at the right and therefore using a plus sign (see page 69), we can write:

$$[HCOH] \xrightarrow[\text{glycolysis}]{\text{anaerobic}} [HCOH]_L + 0.37 \text{ ev}$$

sixth-glucose · · · third-lactic

(Equation 12)

Compare this with the 5 ev of free energy made available by glucose oxidation; that is, by the combination of a sixth-glucose and oxygen to form carbon dioxide and water (see Equation 10). Only 7.5 per cent of the energy made available by the complete oxidation of glucose is made available by the partial breakdown involved in anaerobic glycolysis.

The remaining 92.5 per cent of the free energy remains in the lactic acid molecules, and can be liberated when those molecules are completely oxidized. Placed in terms of third-lactic, we have:

$$[\text{HCOH}]_L + O_2 \longrightarrow CO_2 + H_2O + 4.63 \text{ ev}$$

(Equation 13)

Suppose we consider Equations 12 and 13 together. The third-lactic which is produced in Equation 12 is consumed in Equation 13 and may therefore be "cancelled out"; that is, eliminated from both equations. Adding the rest, we find that $[\text{HCOH}] + O_2 \longrightarrow CO_2 + H_2O + 5$ ev.

In other words, Equation 12 + Equation 13 = Equation 10. This is made necessary by the laws of conservation of matter and of energy. Of course, the universe doesn't have to obey these laws, which are man-made, but it apparently seems to. Whenever such additions of chemical equations can be tested experimentally, it is invariably found that the predictions of the laws are correct.

Now we can show the carbon cycle as involving the addition of anaerobic glycolysis and oxidation on the down-hill side, with oxygen involved only in the latter (see Figure 14).

Anaerobic glycolysis seems terribly inefficient since it produces only about 1/13 of the free energy that could be liberated by total oxidation. This apparent inefficiency is, however, more than made up for by the fact that anaerobic glycolysis has the great saving grace of requiring no oxygen.

Muscle tissue must, in many an emergency, draw on large energy stores when time is lacking for the machinery of the body to bring oxygen to the spot in the necessary quantities. The muscle then makes use of anaerobic glycolysis.

Once the emergency is over, a small fraction of the lactic acid can be completely oxidized and the relatively large quantity of free energy thus made available will suffice to convert the remaining lactic acid back to glucose first, and then glycogen.

With respect to oxygen, the muscle "flies now and pays later."

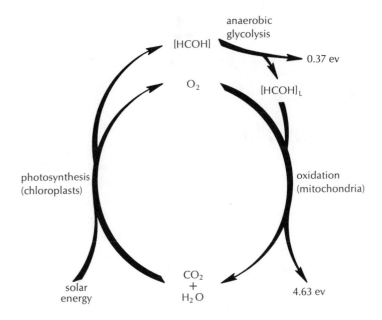

Figure 14. The Carbon Cycle (with Anaerobic Glycolysis)

4

The Intermediates of the Cycle

A New Element

Even though anaerobic glycolysis makes available only 1/13 of the free energy change involved in the total oxidation of glucose to carbon dioxide and water, that fraction is still too much. For each glucose molecule split into two lactic acid molecules, 2.25

ev are made available. To use that, all in one piece, to form bonds requiring an investment of 0.1 ev or so, would certainly be wasteful. The body can, and does, do better.

Anaerobic glycolysis does not, in fact, take place in a single step. In converting glucose to lactic acid, living tissue goes through a number of steps which, as a group, we may call the "glycolytic chain." In the muscle, then, or in any tissue in which anaerobic glycolysis takes place, there must be present a number of other substances that are neither glucose nor lactic acid. Each of these substances is formed in a particular step of the glycolytic chain and is then used up in the succeeding step, disappearing, so to speak, as quickly as it appears.

The chemical changes that regularly take place in living tissue, in order that those tissues may perform their function, are lumped together under the general term "metabolism." The change from glucose to lactic acid is a part of "glucose metabolism," for instance. The substances that appear and disappear on the way from glucose to lactic acid are examples of "metabolic intermediates."

Because metabolic intermediates are consumed as they are produced, the quantity present at any moment in the tissues is very small. (Thus, it is possible that 20,000 men needing haircuts may enter a particular barber-shop in the course of a year and 20,000 men no longer needing haircuts may leave in the course of a year, but at any particular moment, there may be no more than three or four men in the barber-shop.) So little of each intermediate is present, in fact, that their existence remained unknown prior to the twentieth century.

The first indication that such short-lived intermediates existed came in 1905, and laid the groundwork for the later working out of the glycolytic chain by Meyerhof.

In 1905, two English chemists, Arthur Harden and W. J. Young, were studying the manner in which yeast cells broke down glucose molecules to alcohol and carbon dioxide, a process called "fermentation." This is actually a form of anaerobic glycolysis and was discovered, eventually, to be quite similar to what took place in muscle. The process in yeast cells went one step farther, however. The lactic acid that was formed was broken down to alcohol and carbon dioxide:

$$C_3H_6O_3 \longrightarrow C_2H_6O + CO_2$$

lactic	ethyl	carbon
acid	alcohol	dioxide

(Equation 14)

The progress of the reaction could be followed easily by the rate of appearance of carbon dioxide bubbles. After fermentation had continued for a while, the rate of bubbling decreased. This meant the yeast cells were slowing down on their job, either because they were dying or because some substance, essential to the job, was coming into short supply. (After all, the yeast cells were multiplying as fermentation proceeded and each new cell needed new material to work with.)

Harden and Young guessed that something was in short supply. There was still ample glucose, so it had to be something else; some auxiliary material, the nature of which was not obvious. They tried adding different substances to the fermenting mixture in order to see what, if anything, would restore activity. To their rather considerable surprise, they found that the addition of inorganic phosphate compounds would cause the fermenting mixture to bubble with renewed vitality.

This made it clear at once that another element played an important role in the carbon cycle, and every discovery since that turning point in 1905 has made the key importance of that element more obvious.

The element is "phosphorus," a non-metal, symbolized by the letter P. The most familiar phosphorus-containing compound is phosphoric acid, H_3PO_4. Notice that this contains the phosphorus-oxygen combination "PO_4," which is called the "phosphate group." The vast majority of phosphorus compounds found in nature contain it; and, in particular, all the phosphorus compounds associated with living tissue do. Let us agree to represent the phosphate group as "Ph" and we can then write phosphoric acid as H_3Ph.

One, two, or all three of the hydrogen atoms in the phosphoric acid molecule can be replaced by other atoms or groups of atoms and the result is then a "phosphate." If the replacement contains carbon atoms, the result is an "organic phosphate." A carbon-containing group of atoms is often represented, by chemists, with the letter "R." An organic phosphate can therefore be written as RPh. If the replacement does not contain carbon, the result is an "inorganic phosphate." For instance, one of the hydrogen atoms can be replaced by a potassium atom (symbol, K) and that would give us "potassium acid phosphate" or KH_2Ph, an inorganic phosphate.

The importance of inorganic phosphate to life was made clear, to a certain extent, long before the twentieth century. In 1769, a Swedish chemist, Karl Wilhelm Scheele, had discovered that phosphate groups were an important component of the bones of vertebrates, including those of man. In fact, two-thirds of bone is a perfectly inorganic mineral that is, for the most part, a form of calcium phosphate. Since the skeleton is an obviously necessary part of bony vertebrates, it follows that phosphorus is an element essential to vertebrate life, if for no other reason than that.

But this is too conservative a statement. Phosphorus is essential to all parts of the body; to the "soft tissues" as well as to bone. It is essential to plant life, too, and that is notoriously lacking in bone. Indeed, one of the most important chemical fertilizers for the encouragement of plant growth is a form of calcium phosphate.

It was taken for granted, though, throughout the nineteenth century that if phosphorus was essential to life generally, it was essential primarily as inorganic phosphate for that was the only form in which phosphorus compounds were detected in living tissue.

Harden and Young's experiments, however, introduced something new. Inorganic phosphate had been added to the fermenting mixture and the yeast cells perked up. So far, so good. It seemed astonishing that inorganic phosphate should be involved in breaking down glucose, but what was even more astonishing was that the inorganic phosphate did not remain in the solution after it was added. The chemical tests by which Harden and Young measured the quantity of phosphate present showed a steadily declining value as fermentation proceeded.

Naturally, Harden and Young did not for a moment suppose that phosphates were literally disappearing. They understood quite well that chemical tests had their short-comings and limitations. They do not test for a particular atom or group of atoms, but for certain properties characteristic of them. If a group of atoms altered its inner structure in such a way as to lose those properties, the chemical test would record the disappearance of those properties.

In this particular case, Harden and Young were detecting properties characteristic of inorganic phosphates but not of organic phosphates. It became therefore a clear possibility that the yeast cells, in the course of fermentation, converted inorganic phosphate into organic phosphate and that it was the organic phosphate that then played the role in fermentation.

This was not easy to believe for no one had yet had any inkling that organic phosphates could play any part in the machinery of living tissue, or that organic phosphates existed at all in such tissue. To make their point reasonably convincing, Harden and Young felt they had to locate organic phosphates in their fermentation-by-yeast system.

They began to analyze the system for small quantities of any organic compound that might contain phosphate groups and were successful. They found a substance so constructed that not one, but two, phosphate groups were attached to a molecule called "fructose" (quite similar, in properties and structure, to glucose). This molecule is therefore called "fructose diphosphate," although an alternate name, honoring the discoverers, is "Harden-Young ester."

For his work in this field, Harden received a share of the 1929 Nobel Prize in chemistry.

The bond that attaches the phosphate group to the fructose molecule (or to other similar molecules) is quite an ordinary bond. It requires the usual input of free energy for its formation (about 0.1 to 0.2 ev) and it makes available that same usual amount of free energy when the bond is broken.

Not so in every case, however. There are certain organic phosphates in which the phosphate group is hooked to the rest of the molecule in a rather unstable fashion. It is as though the bond has to be stretched, so to speak, to get the phosphate group hooked on. Naturally, more free energy must be invested to form such a phosphate and, correspondingly, more free energy is made available when such a phosphate bond is broken.

These "high-energy phosphates" store amounts of energy that may be as high as 0.5 ev, and it turns out that they are the key intermediates in the utilization of energy in the body. When free energy is made available by the glycolytic chain or any other process, some of it goes into the formation of high-energy phosphates. It is these high-energy phosphates which serve as the "small-denomination bills" referred to on page 75. They represent energy packets of convenient size for utilization by the body, something first made clear by the German-American biochemist Fritz Albert Lipmann in 1941. He received a share of the 1953 Nobel Prize for medicine and physiology as a result.

High-energy phosphates are used, for instance, in the formation of new bonds in the body. By way of such bond formation, the synthesis of proteins and nucleic acids becomes possible, as well as the formation of special compounds required for such processes as nerve conduction, muscle contraction, and kidney filtration.

The high-energy phosphate group does not simply break away from its organic component in order to bring this to pass. If it did so, the energy it released would puff away as heat. Instead, the high-energy phosphate releases its phosphate group to another compound, which becomes a phosphate in its turn.

The second compound requires an input of free energy to become a phosphate. It could not, therefore, become a phosphate merely by being mixed with inorganic phosphate. However, the high-energy phosphate, in releasing its phosphate group, makes available more free energy than is required for the formation of the second phosphate. The high-energy phosphate disappears and in its place is a lower-energy phosphate.

This is a chemical analogy to such familiar physical processes as air entering an automobile tire from a compressed-air tank, or heat entering a kettle of water from a flame beneath, or water entering a trough from an overhead reservoir. This happens because the air in the tank is even more compressed than it is in the tire; the flame is even hotter than the water in the kettle; and the water in the reservoir is higher than the water in the trough. In every case we have a "down-hill" movement, literally so, in the case of the water descending from the reservoir and figuratively so in the case of the air expanding into the tire, and the heat diffusing into the water.

And so it is with the chemical energy of the bonds between atoms. The high-energy phosphate transfers its phosphate group to form a lower-energy phosphate in a "down-hill" movement. For this lower-energy phosphate, any other atom grouping forming a bond of similar energy content can be substituted. Thus, in R-Ph, another R can be substituted for the Ph, to yield R-R. In this way the individual parts of a giant molecule can be put together one at a time, each part adding on through the utilization of a high-energy phosphate.

Naturally, the high-energy phosphates must be replaced as they are consumed, or the body will run down in no time. These high-energy phosphates are, indeed, produced out of the energy released by such processes as anaerobic glycolysis. Indeed, we might almost say that the whole point of anaerobic glycolysis (and of other similar processes) is to form the high-energy phosphates on which the body's economy depends.

Trapping the Energy

The best-known of all the high-energy phosphates was first discovered in 1929 by a German biochemist, K. Lohmann. In that year, he obtained from muscle a compound whose molecule contained a well-known tissue substance called "adenosine." To it were attached three phosphate groups in a short chain so that the compound was called "adenosine triphosphate," a name universally abbreviated as "ATP."

Of the three phosphate groups, it was eventually discovered that the second and third (counting outward from the adenosine) were both high-energy. Under ordinary circumstances, however, only the third and outermost takes part in phosphate group transfer, and it is only that one we need concern ourselves with.

If the outermost phosphate group of ATP is removed or transferred, what is left is adenosine with two phosphate groups. This is "adenosine diphosphate" or "ADP."

It is important to remember that the difference between ADP and ATP is the extra phosphate group in the latter, something that is, alas, obscured in the universal use of the initials. For that reason, I shall write ATP as ADP~Ph, whenever I want to use it in an equation involving phosphate group transfer. Otherwise, it may seem to the casual reader that a phosphate group has appeared out of nowhere—or disappeared into nowhere. The use of the wavy line ($\sim$) indicates that the phosphate group in ADP~Ph is high-energy. A low-energy phosphate would be indicated by the use of an ordinary straight line (-) for its bond.

When ATP loses its high-energy phosphate and becomes ADP, it makes available about 0.3 ev. This is amply sufficient to form ordinary bonds requiring an input of 0.1 or even 0.2 ev.

But exactly how are ATP molecules formed? Tissue supply of this compound, at any one time, is very small and would be consumed in minutes if no more were available. It follows that ATP must be formed in living tissue; formed rapidly and formed continuously.

From what I have said so far in the book, it is clear that the energy supply in living tissue stems from the conversion of glucose to carbon dioxide and water. Somehow, this must result in the formation of ATP. Another way of looking at it is that some of the free energy made available by the conversion of glucose to carbon dioxide and water must be trapped and temporarily "frozen" in the form of ATP. It is only this trapped portion that can be used to drive forward energy-consuming chemical changes —changes that are essential to and inseparable from life.

If that is so, we might suspect that some ATP is formed even in the small portion of glucose metabolism represented by anaerobic glycolysis, which begins with glucose and ends with lactic acid. To see if this is so, let us go through the details of the glycolytic chain (leaving out, I promise you, as many as possible).

We begin with glucose, but if we want a high-energy phosphate, we will need to add a phosphate group. This is done at once. The very first step in the glycolytic chain is to add a phosphate group to glucose, using as the source nothing other than ATP.

To avoid as much of the complication of chemical formulas as possible, let us write glucose, a 6-carbon compound, as simply [6C] in this particular section of the book. And here is a place, also, where we can write ATP as ADP~Ph to make the process of phosphate transfer clearer. The first step in the glycolytic chain can be written then, as:

$$[6C] \; + \; ADP\!\sim\!Ph \; \longrightarrow \; [6C]\text{-}Ph \; + \; ADP$$

glucose-
phosphate

(*Equation 15*)

The glucose-phosphate produced in this reaction cannot be considered a high-energy phosphate for the free energy it makes available on loss of its phosphate group is only about 0.2 ev. That is why a straight line is used in writing [6C]-Ph.

Notice that at 0.3 ev we consider ATP as high-energy; at 0.2 ev glucose-phosphate is low-energy. We might take the dividing line between the two forms as 0.25 ev, but note that this is arbitrary. There is a smooth variation of energy content for various kinds of phosphates and it is only a matter of human convenience to divide them into high- and low-energy groups. In fact, ATP has the lowest energy of the high-energy groups. In fact, ATP has what gives it its key importance, as we shall see.

If you consider Equation 15, then, you will see that we have used up a high-energy phosphate to obtain a low-energy one. We have moved backward. Far from finding that anaerobic glycolysis is producing ATP for tissue use, it is actually consuming it.

There is worse to come. The atoms of the glucose-phosphate molecule rearrange themselves slightly to form the closely similar compound "fructose-phosphate" (still capable of being symbolized as [6C]-Ph). The rearrangement serves the purpose of supplying a position where a second phosphate group can be added, again at the expense of ATP. The new compound is fructose-diphosphate (the compound first discovered by Harden and Young) and it can be written as Ph-[6C]-Ph.

The overall equation we could write for these first few steps of anaerobic glycolysis is:

$$[6C] \; + \; 2ADP\!\sim\!Ph \; \longrightarrow \; Ph\text{-}[6C]\text{-}Ph \; + \; 2ADP$$

(*Equation 16*)

Two molecules of ATP have been consumed to form the two low-energy phosphates in fructose diphosphate.

The next step is the splitting of the fructose-diphosphate in half. In place of a 6-carbon compound with 2 phosphate groups, we end up with two 3-carbon compounds, each with 1 phosphate group:

$$Ph\text{-}[6C]\text{-}Ph \longrightarrow Ph\text{-}[3C] + [3C]\text{-}Ph$$

(Equation 17)

At first the two 3-carbon compounds are slightly different from each other, but a little atomic rearrangement makes them identical. The original molecule of glucose, plus two phosphate groups, has now become two molecules of "glyceraldehyde phosphate." I will give its formula in some detail (see Figure 15) because it will be useful to us. The phosphate group in glyceraldehyde phosphate is lower-energy than ever: about 0.1 ev.

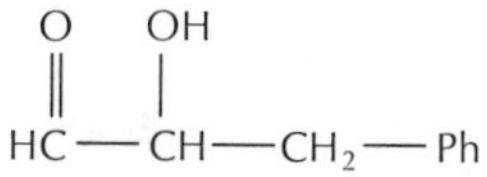

$$
\begin{array}{cc}
O & OH \\
\parallel & \mid \\
HC\!-\!\!\!-\!CH\!\!-\!\!\!-\!CH_2\!-\!\!\!-\!Ph
\end{array}
$$

Figure 15. Glyceraldehyde Phosphate

To the two molecules of glyceraldehyde phosphate, formed from the original glucose molecule, new phosphate groups are added—one to each. These represent the third and fourth phosphate groups added to the carbon atoms originally forming part of the glucose molecule.

This time, however, the addition is done differently. The two previous occasions on which a phosphate group was added, that group replaced a hydroxyl group (OH). This time, however, a phosphate group is to be added to the left-most carbon atom shown in Figure 15, the one that has the structure HC-. To make this possible, we can consider this (somewhat simplified) version of what takes place. A water molecule (H_2O) is added and two hydrogen atoms (2H) then subtracted. This means that an oxygen atom (O) is left behind. The result can be viewed as simply as possible, if we take into account only the left-most carbon of glyceraldehyde phosphate:

$$\overset{\overset{\textstyle O}{\|}}{HC\text{-}} + H_2O \longrightarrow \overset{\overset{\textstyle O}{\|}}{HO\text{-}C\text{-}} + 2H$$

(Equation 18)

Next, the resulting hydroxyl group that has been formed can be viewed as being replaced by a phosphate group, so that the structure becomes Ph-C-. The new compound is diphosphoglyceric acid.

But there is something new here. It is usually easy to attach a phosphate group to a carbon atom which is attached by single bonds to other atoms. The result is then a low-energy phosphate. This is the case in glyceraldehyde phosphate as you can see in Figure 15.

If, however, the phosphate group is attached to a carbon atom which is in turn attached to some other atom by two bonds (a double bond) the phosphate group is put into place with greater difficulty and it is therefore high-energy. This is the case in diphosphoglyceric acid where the phosphate group is attached to a carbon atom which is in turn attached by a double bond to an oxygen atom. Diphosphoglyceric acid is therefore high-energy and must be written as Ph~[3C]-Ph or, in more detail, as shown in Figure 16.

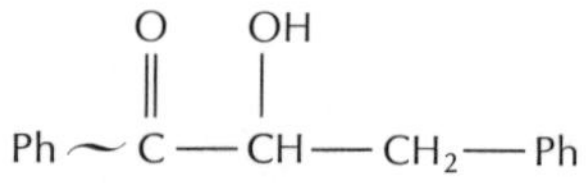

$$Ph \sim \overset{\overset{\textstyle O}{\|}}{C} - \overset{\overset{\textstyle OH}{|}}{CH} - CH_2 - Ph$$

Figure 16. Diphosphoglyceric Acid

But where does the energy come from to form the high-energy phosphate in diphosphoglyceric acid? From ATP? No, indeed, for the new high-energy phosphate here formed requires an input of 0.5 ev, considerably more than the 0.3 ev that ATP can make available. From where, then?

The energy comes in this case from the loss of two hydrogen atoms as indicated in Equation 18. Such a loss of hydrogen ("dehydrogenation") always involves the loss of a particularly large quantity of free energy; free energy that then becomes available for the formation of high-energy phosphates. How much becomes available depends on where the lost hydrogen atoms are transferred. When they are transferred to oxygen atoms, enough free energy is made available to form as many as three high-energy phosphates for every pair of hydrogen atoms transferred.

In anaerobic glycolysis, no oxygen is used and no oxygen is available to accept the hydrogen atoms. The hydrogen atoms are therefore transferred to a compound that occurs later in the glycolytic chain. This reduces the amount of free energy made available, but leaves enough for the formation of one high-energy phosphate, anyway, the one in diphosphoglyceric acid.

Because of this, no special high-energy source for phosphate is needed. The dehydrogenation takes care of it. All that is needed is inorganic phosphate, which we can symbolize as Ph_i. It is low-energy indeed, but that is all right. We can write an equation for the change:

$$[3C]\text{-}Ph + Ph_i \longrightarrow Ph\sim[3C]\text{-}Ph$$

(Equation 19)

Remember now that I said diphosphoglyceric acid could not be formed at the expense of ATP because the high-energy bond in the former required more energy than ATP had at its disposal. The phosphate in diphosphoglyceric acid requires 0.5 ev, while ATP contains only 0.3 ev. But then, matters can be reversed. Diphosphoglyceric acid can be used in forming ATP. The high-energy phosphate group in the former can be transferred to ADP to form ATP, thus:

$$\text{Ph}\!\sim\![3C]\text{-Ph} + \text{ADP} \longrightarrow [3C]\text{-Ph} + \text{ADP}\!\sim\!\text{Ph}$$

$$\textit{(Equation 20)}$$

An 0.5 ev bond is eliminated and an 0.3 ev bond (still high-energy) is formed. The process is "downhill" and takes place easily. This reaction, the first shown to be capable of *producing* ATP, rather than consuming it, was first worked out in 1939 by the German biochemist Otto Heinrich Warburg. (He had already received the Nobel Prize for medicine and physiology in 1931, for his earlier discoveries in the field of glucose metabolism.)

But now we have replaced the high-energy phosphate group in diphosphoglyceric acid with an ordinary hydroxyl group, and the low-energy phosphate group is shifted from the end to the middle-carbon. The result is phosphoglyceric acid (Figure 17), which, like glyceraldehyde phosphate, can be written [3C]-Ph.

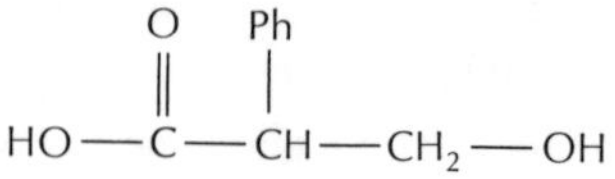

$$\begin{array}{ccc} \text{O} & \text{Ph} & \\ \parallel & | & \\ \text{HO}-\text{C}-\text{CH}-\text{CH}_2 & -\text{OH} \end{array}$$

Figure 17. Phosphoglyceric Acid

The phosphate group in phosphoglyceric acid is low-energy. Can something be done with it? Something can and something is. A hydrogen atom and a hydroxyl group (H + OH) is removed from the compound. Since the hydrogen and hydroxyl, taken together, can be considered as making up a water molecule, such a reaction is said to be a "dehydration." Phosphoglyceric acid is thus converted to another compound, phosphoenolpyruvic acid (Figure 18). If you compare Figure 18 with Figure 17, you will

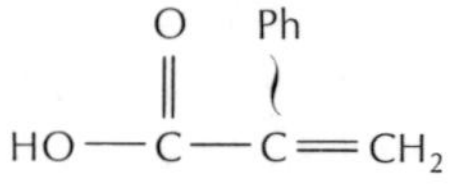

$$\begin{array}{ccc} \text{O} & \text{Ph} & \\ \parallel & | & \\ \text{HO}-\text{C}-\text{C} & = \text{CH}_2 \end{array}$$

Figure 18. Phosphoenolpyruvic Acid

see where the hydrogen atom and the hydroxyl group have been removed.

The removal of the hydrogen and hydroxyl means, however, that a double bond must be formed to satisfy all the valence bonds of the carbon atoms. The phosphate group attached to the compound is thus attached to a carbon atom which is in turn attached to another carbon atom by a double bond. This is a situation which makes the phosphate group in phosphoenolpyruvic acid high-energy, as is shown in Figure 18. The energy input required to convert the low-energy phosphate group in phosphoglyceric acid to the high-energy phosphate group in phosphoenolpyruvic acid is obtained from the free energy made available in the process of the dehydration. We can write then:

$$[3C]\text{-Ph} \longrightarrow [3C]\sim\text{Ph} + H_2O$$

(Equation 21)

The high-energy phosphate in phosphoenolpyruvic acid is high-energy indeed; it has 0.55 ev to make available. Its phosphate group can be transferred to ADP to form ATP without any trouble at all.

$$[3C]\sim\text{Ph} + \text{ADP} \longrightarrow [3C] + \text{ADP}\sim\text{Ph}$$

(Equation 22)

Once the phosphoenolpyruvic acid has transferred its phosphate group, what is left is a 3-carbon compound without a phosphate group, indicated in Equation 22 as [3C]. It is "pyruvic acid," the first compound in the glycolytic chain since glucose itself to be without a phosphate group.

Pyruvic acid differs from lactic acid in having two less hydrogen atoms in its molecule. Pyruvic acid therefore accepts the two hydrogen atoms given up by glyceraldehyde phosphate in an earlier step in the chain (see page 20) and becomes lactic acid, and anaerobic glycolysis is finished.

Now let's go through the chain in the form of an overall diagram; one which does not show every step, by any means, but which gives the major details useful for our purposes. This is shown in Figure 19.

As you see, three chemical changes take place in this scheme (numbered 1 to 3), which alter the original [6C] (glucose) to two [3C]-Ph (glyceraldehyde phosphate). Five more chemical changes are listed in converting each [3C]-Ph to the final lactic acid [3C]. Since these changes are identical for each glyceraldehyde phosphate they are numbered 4a to 8a and 4b to 8b.

Next, let's consider the bookkeeping.

In step 1, an ATP enters the reaction and leaves as ADP, its high-energy phosphate group shorn away. In step 2, the same thing happens. This means that two ATP molecules have been consumed and two ADP molecules have been formed. However, in steps 5a and 5b an ADP is, in each case, consumed and an ATP is formed. Therefore, 5a and 5b exactly cancel 1 and 2, and both can be eliminated from any consideration of the overall change.

In step 4a and 4b a molecule of water is, in each case, added to the system, but in step 6a and 6b a molecule of water is, in each case, removed from the system. In 4a and 4b two hydrogen atoms are, in each case, removed from the system, but in steps 8a and 8b two hydrogen atoms are, in each case, added to the system. Both the water molecule and the two hydrogen atoms can therefore be eliminated from any consideration in weighing the overall change.

There are only two sets of changes which are not cancelled out. In steps 4a and 4b inorganic phosphate is, in each case, added to the system and nowhere is it removed. Then in steps 7a and 7b a molecule of ADP enters the system and a molecule of ATP leaves it. This is not balanced either. The overall change in anaerobic glycolysis can therefore be written as follows:

$$C_6H_{12}O_6 + 2Ph_i + 2\ ADP \longrightarrow 2C_3H_6O_3 + 2ADP{\sim}Ph + 1.65\ ev$$
glucose   lactic acid

(Equation 23)

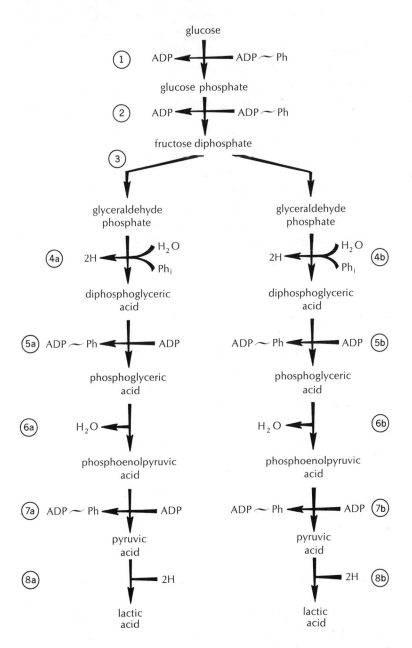

Figure 19. The Glycolytic Chain

Notice that in this reaction there is a loss in free energy from the system to the outer world of 1.65 ev. This means the reaction is "down-hill" and can proceed spontaneously. However, the conversion of a molecule of glucose to lactic acid without the intervention of phosphate groups results in a free energy loss of 2.25 ev (see page 77). In short, living tissue manages to salvage 0.6 ev and put that into the useful form of two molecules of ATP.

This is done very ingeniously and yet the results may seem disappointing. Only about one-fourth of the energy available in anaerobic glycolysis is caught in the ATP trap. The rest is gone and, apparently, wasted. Must this be so? Or is it just that anaerobic glycolysis is an inherently inefficient way of producing useful energy. To settle that matter let's pass on to glucose oxidation; that is, its combination with oxygen—which produces far more energy than glycolysis does.

Giving up the Hydrogen

In considering glucose oxidation, let's begin with lactic acid and follow it through to carbon dioxide and water. The first step is a reversal of the last step of glycolysis. That is, two hydrogen atoms are withdrawn from lactic acid, converting it to pyruvic acid.

Yet, this is more than mere reversal. In anaerobic glycolysis molecular oxygen was not involved. If two hydrogen atoms were removed in steps 4a and 4b of the glycolytic chain (see Figure 19) then they were restored to that chain in steps 8a and 8b. The removal of hydrogen atoms from lactic acid is a reversal of steps 8a and 8b and to make the reversal complete, those hydrogen atoms should be restored to the chain through a reversal of steps 4a and 4b.

This does not happen. The dehydrogenation of lactic acid, as a first step in the process I am about to describe, is not a true reversal of the glycolytic chain. The hydrogen atoms go elsewhere and we will leave the question of where in abeyance for a moment, and move on.

Both lactic acid and pyruvic acid are 3-carbon compounds. All the significant compounds in the glycolytic chain are either 6-carbon or 3-carbon. Now, however, something new is added. Pyruvic acid not only loses two hydrogen atoms but a molecule of carbon dioxide (CO_2) as well. The molecule of carbon dioxide carries one carbon away and what is left of the molecule contains only two carbon atoms. Indeed, for quite a while, what was left was referred to as the "2-carbon fragment." Its nature was eventually determined, however, and it is now called the "acetyl group."

(Actually, the acetyl group does not exist by itself. As it is formed it joins a rather complicated substance called "coenzyme A" which passes it on further. There are, in fact, enzymes and coenzymes involved at every step of metabolism, the former being large protein molecules and the latter comparatively small molecules that are nevertheless considerably more complicated than glucose, for instance. I am omitting any detailed consideration of enzymes and coenzymes since they will lead me too far off-course, but I do so with considerable guilt feelings.)

The 2-carbon acetyl group combines with a 4-carbon compound called "oxaloacetic acid" and together they make up a 6-carbon compound called "citric acid."

In the course of several chemical changes, citric acid loses first one CO_2 molecule, and then a second, to be reduced to a 4-carbon compound again, and this is eventually converted to oxaloacetic acid once more. The oxaloacetic acid molecule is ready to join with another acetyl group and repeat the process.

Indeed, we are dealing with a cycle, an endlessly repeated series of changes from oxaloacetic acid back to oxaloacetic acid, and at each turn of the cycle an acetyl group is oxidized.

The details of this cycle were worked out in the late 1930's by the German-British biochemist Hans Adolf Krebs, and for it he received a share of the 1953 Nobel Prize for physiology and medicine. In his honor the cycle is often called the "Krebs cycle."

Figure 20 gives an outline scheme of the major steps of the Krebs cycle. Nine chemical changes are listed and numbered in the diagram. We begin with lactic acid, a 3-carbon compound

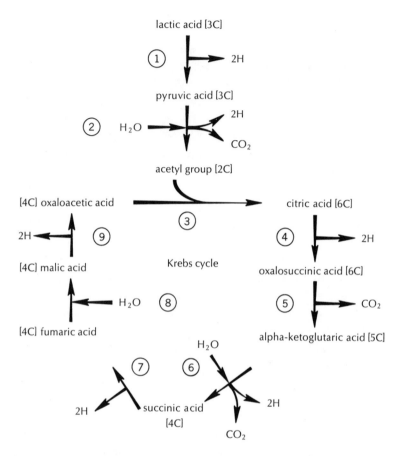

Figure 20. The Oxidation of Lactic Acid

and, in the course of the reactions shown in the diagram, three molecules of CO_2 are formed, at steps 2, 5, and 6. All three carbons of the lactic acid are gone and nothing is left.

Indeed, less than nothing, it might seem. The original lactic acid, with its empirical formula of $C_3H_6O_3$, has six hydrogen atoms. However, there are six places in the diagram (at steps 1, 2, 4, 6, 7, and 9) where a pair of hydrogen atoms are given off. Twelve hydrogen atoms are lost altogether. How can six hydrogen atoms become twelve?

Ah, but notice also that at three places (at steps 2, 6 and 8) a molecule of water is added. Three molecules of water ($3H_2O$) contain six hydrogen atoms and these, added to lactic acid's six, bring the total to twelve.

Furthermore, the three water molecules contribute a total of three oxygen atoms. These are necessary to form the carbon dioxide. The three carbon dioxide molecules produced in the course of the reactions shown in Figure 20 contain six atoms of oxygen altogether ($3CO_2$), of which only three can come from the original lactic acid molecule. The other three must come from the water molecules.

We can therefore set up the following overall formula for the fate of a molecule of lactic acid passing through the Krebs cycle:

$$C_3H_6O_3 + 3H_2O \longrightarrow 3CO_2 + 12H$$

(Equation 24)

But each glucose molecule gives rise to *two* lactic acid molecules. We then have the following overall reaction for the lactic acid arising from a single glucose molecule:

$$2\ C_3H_6O_3 + 6H_2O \longrightarrow 6CO_2 + 24H$$

(Equation 25)

Several questions may now arise:

1. What happens to the 24 hydrogen atoms produced by the breakdown of two molecules of lactic acid arising from a single glucose molecule? Surely, they aren't given off as hydrogen molecules. There is no trace of hydrogen formation by any form of life other than certain bacteria.

2. At what point is the energy produced?

3. At what point do phosphate groups enter the picture? Where is the necessary ATP formed?

Actually, all three questions can be answered once we remember that the Krebs cycle is an *aerobic* breakdown; one that consumes oxygen. (There are experimental techniques which can measure the oxygen consumption with considerable accuracy.)

It is reasonable to suppose that the 24 hydrogen atoms are not "given off" but are transferred from the organic compounds of the Krebs cycle to oxygen atoms, forming water. Twenty-four hydrogen atoms will combine with 12 oxygen atoms (or six oxygen molecules: $6O_2$) to form 12 water molecules.

Note that in Equation 25 we are adding six water molecules to the system. By properly combining the hydrogen atoms also produced, we form 12 water molecules. Six of the water molecules we form cancel the six we put in, leaving a "net" formation of six. We can write Equation 25 in a new form to take the oxygen atoms into account:

$$2C_3H_6O_3 + 6O_2 \longrightarrow 6CO_2 + 6H_2O$$

(Equation 26)

And it is precisely from this process—the transfer of hydrogen atoms from organic compounds to oxygen, forming water—that energy is produced.

The combination of two molecules of lactic acid with oxygen to form carbon dioxide and water (as pictured in Equation 26) involves a free energy loss of 27.6 ev. The transfer of a pair of hydrogen atoms from an organic compound to oxygen involves a free energy loss of 2.25 ev. Where 24 hydrogen atoms are involved, twelve pairs, the free energy loss is 2.25×12 or 27 ev.

Virtually all the energy, then, which is made available to living tissue by lactic acid combination, is made available at precisely those points where the transfer of hydrogen atoms is accomplished. This is something that might be guessed to begin with, really, for a jet of hydrogen burning in oxygen yields an intensely hot flame. The Krebs cycle burns hydrogen slowly and under carefully controlled conditions, and energy is developed in that way just as though the hydrogen were burning in open air.

The difference is that whereas in open air the energy of burning hydrogen is given off completely as heat (plus a little light), the energy of "burning" hydrogen in the Krebs cycle is trapped, to a certain extent, as chemical energy—in the form of ATP.

Perhaps that seems overdoing it a little, though. If 98 per cent of the total free energy loss in the oxidation of lactic acid is crowded into hydrogen transfer and water formation, what about carbon dioxide?

Carbon dioxide is also formed in the oxidation of lactic acid and is there not energy formed when carbon dioxide is produced? When carbon (coal, for instance) is burned in air, quantities of heat are certainly produced. Why shouldn't it be produced in living tissue, when carbon is "burned" to form carbon dioxide?

It would be, if carbon were burned, but it isn't. When carbon dioxide is produced in chemical reactions within the body, it is detached from a molecule in which the carbon is already in combination with oxygen atoms. An example of this is the reaction labelled 5 in Figure 20, where oxalosuccinic acid is converted into alpha-ketoglutaric acid. What happens there is shown in Figure 21.

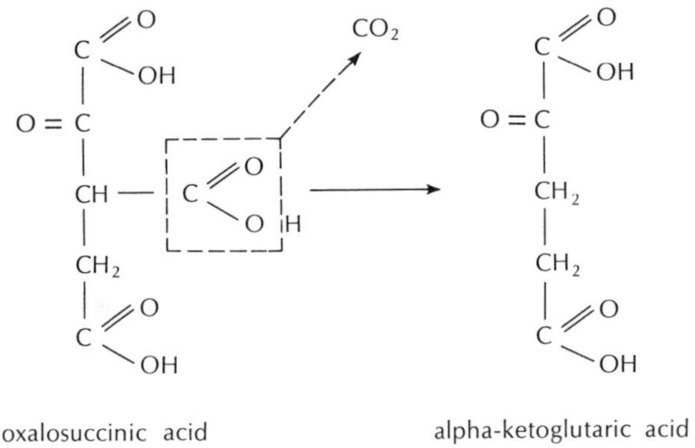

oxalosuccinic acid   alpha-ketoglutaric acid

Figure 21. Decarboxylation

The carbon dioxide is not formed by a combination of carbon with molecular oxygen; that would indeed produce a large free energy loss. Rather it is merely detached from the molecule ("de-carboxylation") where it is already essentially in being. If a carbon atom is attached only to a single oxygen atom, a molecule of water is added to the organic compound ("hydration") and the oxygen atom from the water molecule supplies the second atom for the carbon.

Neither decarboxylation nor hydration involves much of a free energy loss. To repeat—molecular oxygen is not involved in CO_2 formation, but only in H_2O formation, and it is in the latter step that virtually all the free energy loss is concentrated.

But that still leaves us our third question. Where do the phosphate groups come in? Where is ATP?

Clearly, if all the energy is produced in the transfer of hydrogen atoms to oxygen atoms the ATP must be produced in the course of that process, somehow.

The process of transferring hydrogen to oxygen is not, after all, a simple one. Oxygen is a very active substance and, in general, active substances, by their very nature, bring about a variety of chemical changes in whatever they touch. The delicately-balanced structure of living tissue cannot tolerate haphazard changes and active substances are, therefore, dangerous poisons for the most part.

That molecular oxygen can be tolerated by living tissue despite its active nature is entirely owing to the manner in which tissues have evolved a highly specialized system for handling oxygen. The reactions of the Krebs cycle take place entirely within the mitochondria which are the oxygen-handling portions of the cell. Any system making use of molecular oxygen is to be found in the mitochondria and nowhere else. In the mitochondria an entire system of enzymes and coenzymes exists for the central purpose of dealing with atmospheric oxygen in such a way as to keep it tame and harmless at every step.

(There are some microorganisms which get their energy entirely by chemical reactions that do not involve molecular oxygen. They lack mitochondria and for them oxygen is indeed poisonous. They are the "obligate anaerobes." They are, in other words, obligated to make use of anaerobic—non-oxygen—reactions and must live in the absence of oxygen. There are also microorganisms that are "facultative anaerobes"; they can live without oxygen or with oxygen. They do have mitochondria, of course.)

One way in which molecular oxygen can prove poisonous is just this. It has the tendency to combine with hydrogen atoms of organic compounds to form hydrogen peroxide (H_2O_2). This substance in turn interferes with many chemical processes vital to life and is therefore poisonous in small quantities.

Oxygen molecules seem to have a tendency to do this because it is, so to speak, the lazy way out. The two oxygen atoms of the oxygen molecule (O=O) need not separate, but can add on two hydrogen atoms while still hanging together to form hydrogen peroxide (H–O–O–H).

To form water, which is harmless to tissues in reasonable quantities, the oxygen molecule must somehow separate into single atoms, each of which adds on two hydrogen atoms to form water (H–O–H).

A particular enzyme in the mitochondria, "cytochrome oxidase" (containing heme—see page 49—as part of its molecule) has the ability to bring about such a molecular split and the consequent combination of molecular oxygen with hydrogen to form water and *not* hydrogen peroxide. That is the key to the de-fusing, so to speak, of oxygen's poisonous quality. By consuming molecular oxygen in this fashion, and converting it to water, as fast as it is brought into the cells—and using the reaction as a major source of energy besides—the fangs of the serpent are drawn.

The hydrogen atoms released within the mitochondria, in the course of the Krebs cycle, combine with oxygen under the influence of cytochrome oxidase—but not immediately. They are passed from hand to hand, so to speak, by a series of relatively complex substances (making up the "cytochrome system"), each of which is capable of accepting the two hydrogen atoms from the one before itself in line and passing it on to the one after itself.

This passage from one member of the cytochrome system to the next is a "downhill" process. With each transfer there is a loss of free energy, until the total loss of 2.25 ev made available by the overall passage of a pair of hydrogen atoms from an organic compound to an oxygen atom is accounted for.

Several of the transfer points involve a sufficiently large free energy loss to make possible the "uphill" production of a molecule of ATP from ADP. Generally, there are three such places in the transfer-chain; on rare occasions as many as four, or only two.

Compare this with the situation in glycolysis where the removal of two hydrogen atoms must be followed by their restoration at another point in the chain, since oxygen is lacking. Under these conditions only one ATP molecule is formed.

The use of oxygen thus makes available to tissue an extraordinarily rich potential source of ATP. It is this that makes it so useful for tissues to possess mechanisms for safely handling that ubiquitously available, but active and dangerous substance, oxygen.

The process whereby hydrogen atoms are oxidized, that is, combined with oxygen to form water, while ADP is, at the same time, "phosphorylated," that is, given another phosphate group to form ATP, is referred to as "oxidative phosphorylation."

The details of oxidative phosphorylation—the actual reactions that connect the "downhill" slide of hydrogen atoms along the cytochrome system with the "uphill" movement of phosphate groups from ADP to ATP—are still not worked out. It takes place, though, whatever the details, and it is this which is the chief source of tissue energy in almost every form of life.

The Energy Roller-coaster

If you look back at Figure 20 on page 98, you will see that a pair of hydrogen atoms are given off at steps 1, 2, 4, 6, 7, and 9. Of these, the dehydrogenations at 1, 2, 4, and 9 result in the production of three molecules of ATP each. Step 6 produces four and step 7 produces only two. Altogether, then, each molecule of lactic acid, in the course of its oxidation to carbon dioxide and water, produces 18 molecules of ATP.

Suppose, though, we start with glucose. In converting a mole-

cule of glucose to two molecules of lactic acid by anaerobic glycolysis, two molecules of ATP are formed. Each of the pair of
molecules of lactic acid formed from glucose produces eighteen
molecules of ATP in the course of the Krebs cycle. We conclude,
then, that in combining glucose and oxygen to form carbon dioxide
and water, living tissue makes available to itself 2 + 18 + 18,
or 38 molecules of ATP for each molecule of glucose broken
down.

(For each single carbon atom in glucose—for each sixth-glucose, that is—38/6 or 6 1/3 molecules of ATP are formed; 1/3
molecule in the course of anaerobic glycolysis and 6 in the course
of the Krebs cycle. It is a little uncomfortable to speak of a third
of an ATP molecule, but no more so than to speak of a sixth of a
glucose molecule and I am still anxious to keep things on a one-
carbon-atom basis.)

The 38 molecules of ATP represent a store of free energy equal
to 38 × 0.3, or 11.4 ev, although the total oxidation of a glucose
molecule to carbon dioxide and water represents a free energy
loss of 29.8 ev. In short, living tissue manages to salvage about
38 per cent (11.4/29.8) of the free energy ideally made available in glucose oxidation.

The remaining 62 per cent of the free energy is converted into
heat. Some of this is specifically useful, to warm-blooded creatures
such as mammals and birds, for it keeps body temperature at a
favorable and comparatively high point (roughly 100° F.) though
the outside temperature may be quite cold. Nevertheless, even
in warm-blooded creatures, most of the heat produced in glucose
oxidation must be disposed of into the surrounding atmosphere.

Some is gotten rid of by radiation, but the rate of radiation
is not usually great enough to do the job. The human skin, for
instance, has numerous sweat glands that secrete perspiration
(which is almost entirely water). The perspiration covers the body
in a thin film and is evaporated, usually, as quickly as it is produced, so that the skin feels reasonably dry. The conversion of
liquid perspiration into water-vapor is an energy-consuming reaction, and the energy required for the task is withdrawn from

the skin beneath, cooling the body at a much higher rate than ordinary radiation would manage.

Loss of heat by radiation depends on the difference in temperatures between the heat-donor (the body) and the heat-acceptor (the atmosphere). When the air temperature rises, radiation is cut down and a greater load is placed on perspiration-evaporation. The rate of perspiration production must increase.

The same is true after exercise, when larger quantities of glucose are oxidized and more heat is produced. Radiation cannot be increased unless the body temperature rises, which is undesirable. The rate of perspiration is increased instead.

With temperature rise and exercise, perspiration may be produced faster than it can evaporate, particularly if the atmosphere is humid. We then sweat visibly and our discomfort under such conditions is the best evidence we have of the less than 40 per cent efficiency of our energy storage in glucose oxidation.

Inefficiency of this sort is found, in fact, at every step of energy transfer. It is like transferring water from container to container to container in our cupped hands. Some water is going to leak away at each step.

Suppose we consider anaerobic glycolysis, for instance. The conversion of a molecule of glucose to two molecules of lactic acid involves a free energy loss of 2.25 ev and out of this, two high-energy phosphates are produced. We can say, therefore, that it takes 1.12 ev of free energy loss in the conversion of glucose to lactic acid to form a single high-energy phosphate.

If we consider phosphoenolpyruvic acid as the high-energy phosphate formed (see page 92), we find the free energy stored in the formation of one molecule of this compound to be 0.55 ev. It is then used to form a molecule of ATP from ADP which involves a storage of 0.3 ev, and the ATP is then utilized to form ordinary chemical bonds of tissue-substances which represent a free energy storage of 0.1 to 0.2 ev per bond.

We can represent this in Figure 22.

Notice that the energy-transfer scheme shown in Figure 22

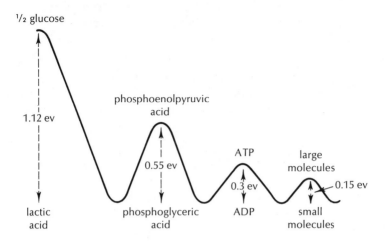

Figure 22. The Energy Roller-coaster

strongly resembles a roller-coaster, for in a mechanical roller-coaster, each rise is lower than the rise before.

It may bother our sense of neatness and conservationism to have energy transfers proceed so inefficiently, but the inefficiency is necessary. It is the inefficiency that drives the whole process, and we can see this if we actually consider a mechanical roller-coaster.

In order for a drop to supply the energy needed to send a car up the next rise of a roller-coaster, the previous drop must be higher than the subsequent rise. If a roller-coaster were designed with all the peaks at equal heights, the car would go swooping down the first drop and then would fail to make the top of the next rise, because of energy losses through friction, air resistance and so on. The car would come to a stop before reaching the top of the next rise and would roll back. Then, after a series of oscillations, it would come to rest in the valley between the first two rises to the chagrin and loudly-expressed indignation of the riders.

The same for the energy roller-coaster. If each energy peak were as high as the one before, the energy represented by the first fall would not be sufficient to drive the molecule up to the next peak, thanks to inevitable losses through entropy increase.

It is gravity that drives the roller-coaster and, essentially, the car is sliding down a slope that can be imagined by drawing a line through the topmost points of all the rises. The steeper the slope, the faster the overall ride (although by making peaks and valleys, one makes the ride faster-than-average at some points at the cost of making it slower-than-average at others).

In the same way it is overall free-energy loss (obtained by imagining a line through the tops of the rises) which keeps the energy roller-coaster running. If the energy transfer were 100 per cent efficient and all the tops were at the same height, the line through them would be level and the whole process would stop, as it would in a mechanical roller-coaster.

The energy roller-coaster must avoid either of two extremes. It can't be too steep. That is, the initial free energy drop from a half-molecule of glucose to lactic acid cannot be used directly to form a single protein bond which is all that is formed in the end. If it were, the reaction would be too difficult to reverse. It takes energy to reconvert lactic acid to glucose (something tissue must be able to do) and if that energy must be added all in one big packet, the process becomes impractical. By making the energy roller-coaster a gentle slope, in a number of steps, lactic acid can be converted to glucose by successive additions of relatively small quantities of energy, something the body can handle easily.

On the other hand, if the energy roller-coaster has a slope that is too gentle; if there are too many steps interposed with very little difference in heights; the overall reaction would move far too slowly for the body's good.

The actual situation, as shown in Figure 22 is, presumably, a happy compromise between the two extremes; the one that works best.

Some writers, concentrating on the last rise in Figure 22, suggest that life manages to "reverse the direction of entropy change," and that it is the ability to do so that defines life. They point out that living tissue begins with small molecules and builds up large intricate molecules such as those of protein and nucleic acid; and, what's more, keeps them in existence in tissue as long as life persists there. The large molecules contain more free energy than the small ones do and, therefore, less entropy. (Remember that more free energy is always equivalent to less entropy, while less free energy is invariably equivalent to more entropy.)

Since the processes that proceed spontaneously in the Universe move always (as far as we know) in one direction of increasing entropy, or decreasing free energy, the continuous formation of large molecules from small in living tissue is a continuous movement in the direction of decreasing entropy. There is the "reversal."

But this is so only if we concentrate on that last rise in the energy roller-coaster. Let's look at the whole picture, though. Living tissue does form large molecules from small ones but only at the expense of ATP, and the entropy increase in ATP breakdown is greater than the entropy decrease in living tissue. Of course, tissue forms ATP, too, but at the expense of phosphoenolpyruvic acid; and it forms that, too, but at the expense of the glucose conversion to lactic acid.

Living creatures do not defy the second law of thermodynamics. They manage a local entropy decrease in their tissues only at the expense of a much larger entropy increase in their food. Take life and food *together* and entropy goes up.

A second and more subtle point can be made though. In the course of evolution, simple creatures have evolved into complex creatures. Is this not an *overall* decrease in entropy?

It might perhaps be so, if the simple creatures really disappeared as complex creatures formed and if only an increasingly complex set of creatures existed on earth in successive geologic epochs.

Instead, simple creatures remain and complex creatures exist in smaller total quantities than they. Indeed, you can consider life as consisting of a hierarchy of simple creatures, more complex creatures, still more complex creatures, even more complex creatures and so on and so on, with each step upward represented by a smaller total weight of living tissue.

This is another version of the energy roller-coaster. By and large, complex creatures live by eating smaller creatures which eat still smaller creatures and so on. For instance, sharks eat large fish which eat small fish which eat minnows which eat larvae which eat one-celled microorganisms.

But the food a creature eats is turned into its own tissue only as a result of the energy roller-coaster, so that only a small portion of the free energy of the food is stored in the eater's tissues; the rest is wasted.

It is considered a rough rule of thumb that it takes ten pounds of food to build up one pound of tissue, the other nine pounds of food vanishing as heat and material waste.

Therefore there must be a lopsided balance. For each pound of living shark, there must always be 10 pounds of living large fish, and these in turn require 100 pounds of living small fish, which require 1,000 pounds of living minnows, which require 10,000 pounds of living larvae, which require 100,000 pounds of living one-celled microorganisms.

This is an energy roller-coaster too, if you like. The marvellously complex living organism that is the shark maintains its life at the cost of the breakdown of 100,000 times its own weight in the very simple microorganisms. The increased complexity is more than matched by this colossal breakdown, however, and entropy must be viewed as increased overall.

(To be sure, by shortening the food chain, very large creatures can exist in numbers that would be otherwise impossible. The largest whales and sharks, for instance, live on tiny creatures, cutting out three or four steps in the chain. The blue whale—the largest animal ever to have lived on earth—lives almost entirely on tiny shrimp called "krill" which it strains out of sea-water by means of the strips of whalebone in its huge mouth. As a result, a thousand blue whales can exist for every one that could exist, if they tried to live on somewhat smaller whales. Similarly, one hears it said sometimes that if the human population continues to rise, men will have to learn to live on one-celled creatures such as yeast and algae.)

But a third, still more subtle point can be made. Man's civilization involves a massive entropy decrease as he turns ore into raw metal and then into machinery; wood into paper and then into books; chemicals into concrete and then into structures. One might argue at once that this is all accomplished at the cost of a much larger increase in entropy through muscular effort, the burning of coal and oil and so on.

True as far as physical activity is concerned, but what about intellectual activity? How much of an entropy decrease is involved in converting disorganized splotches of color into an inspiring painting; chaotic sounds into a magnificent symphony; random words into a great literary work; aimless thoughts into a startling new concept.

Physicists draw back here. The concept of entropy is applied by them to energy transfer and nothing else. The energy transfer involved in turning random words into "King Lear" is something that can't be measured by ordinary physical methods.

(However, a new branch of mathematics, called "information theory," makes use of the concept of entropy in startling new ways. This may eventually help us determine whether the intellectual activity of mankind can be viewed as succeeding in violating the second law of thermodynamics.)

With the contents of this chapter in mind, it is time to draw a picture of the carbon cycle once again. Ideally, on the downhill side of the cycle we ought now to include every chemical reaction in anaerobic glycolysis and the Krebs cycle. To do so would unbearably complicate the cycle, however, and I won't do it.

I shall instead continue to include only those steps that I think will help demonstrate the essentials of the cycle. Therefore, in Figure 23, the carbon cycle is represented as a roller-coaster, but with only one rise (that involving ATP) indicated.

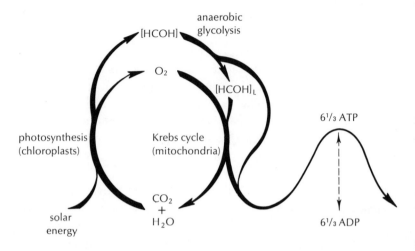

Figure 23. The Carbon Cycle (with Energy Roller-coaster)

5

The Driving Force of the Cycle

The Generous Sun

The picture of the energy roller-coaster shown in Figure 22 (see page 107) inevitably leads to the question: But what brings everything to the top of the highest rise in the first place?

A similar question might be asked about a mechanical roller-coaster. How does the car get to the first and highest rise on which all else depends? In this case, the car is slowly pulled upward at the cost of the energy supplied by a laboring motor. The entropy increase involved in the motor's workings is considerably greater than the entropy decrease brought about by the raising of the car to its peak height. The overall entropy still increases. What's more, the motor does its work at the expense of the electrical energy fed into it, which is created at the expense of the burning fuel, with entropy increasing at each stop. Thus, to the left of the mechanical roller-coaster, if it is viewed schematically something like the picture shown in Figure 22, there is attached an energy roller-coaster.

Indeed, if the electric supply that runs the motor is produced, let us say, by burning coal or oil, then the energy roller-coaster is precisely the one we are concerned with in this book, for coal and oil are the products of plant life that flourished in the far distant past. They arose, indirectly, from carbon cycles that turned several hundred million years ago.

Well, then, what replaces the glucose at the top of the left-

113

most rise in Figure 22 in order to keep the energy roller-coaster (*and* the mechanical roller-coaster) going? As was made plain in the early part of this book, it is the energy of sunlight, exerted through the photosynthetic reaction, that forms the glucose.

It is time, then, to begin considering sunlight in detail.

First, how much sunlight is there? Is there really enough to keep all of life going?

Careful measurements of the amount of energy received by the earth from the Sun has yielded a value for what is called the "solar constant," which is 1.94 calories per square centimeter per minute.

This means that a square centimeter of the earth's surface, exposed to the vertical rays of the Sun (with its radiation undiminished by clouds or haze or even, ideally, by the atmosphere itself) would receive each minute 1.94 calories or, what is equivalent, 50,000,000,000,000,000,000 ev.

If this energy could be used, with perfect efficiency, to turn carbon dioxide and water into glucose and oxygen, then something like 1/56,000 of an ounce of glucose would be formed. This doesn't sound like much, but it is only over one square centimeter of area and over one minute of time. Suppose we considered one square mile of area, instead, over half an hour of time. That is still not a large area on a planetary scale, nor a long time.

It turns out that the solar energy received by one square mile of the earth's surface for half an hour would, if utilized with perfect efficiency, produce 435 *tons* of glucose.

If we took the solar energy received by the entire earth (which has a cross-sectional area of 50 million square miles) then there is enough solar energy to produce 215,000,000,000 tons of glucose in ten hours. This is easily more, in terms of energy, than all the world's animal life would require in a year.

There is no question, then, that solar energy is sufficient for life's needs. We can allow for the fact that clouds and other atmospheric phenomena block off some of the radiation; that much of the radiation falls upon desert areas or mountain tops or polar wastes where plant life does not exist to make use of it; that even when plants do make use of solar energy, they do so inefficiently; that plants must replace not only the quantity of tissue eaten by animals but the quantity that falls prey to decay by microorganisms. Even so, there is clearly enough solar energy for the purpose.

The sheer quantity of the energy supplied to the earth by the generous Sun is impressive. It becomes even more so when we stop to realize that what the earth receives is the merest trifle compared to *all* the energy the Sun emits.

The Sun's energy radiates outward in all directions and only a small fraction happens to hit the Earth; a tiny target indeed, since it is only 8,000 miles across and 93,000,000 miles away. The Earth intercepts only half a billionth of the Sun's total radiating energy.

But where does all that energy come from?

The Sun consists mostly of hydrogen, the simplest of all atoms, with a nucleus made up of a single particle called a proton. Under the terrific temperatures and pressures of the Sun's interior, four of these hydrogen nuclei can fuse together to form a helium nucleus.

This process of "nuclear fusion" liberates enormous quantities of energy. It is hydrogen fusion that powers the terrible hydrogen bomb so that the Sun can be looked upon as a vast hydrogen bomb in continuous explosion, close enough to us to give us light and heat, and far enough away from us to do us no harm (thanks to our blanket of atmosphere which absorbs the worst of the radiation).

We can compare the energy produced by nuclear fusion with that produced by ordinary chemical reactions.

If two hydrogen atoms combine with an oxygen atom to form water, only the particles (electrons) at the very outskirts of the atom are involved. The free energy loss involved is, as we have already seen, about 2.25 ev.

If, however, four hydrogen nuclei fuse to form a helium nucleus, this involves particles at the very center of the atoms. The free energy loss involved in the formation of a single helium atom by fusion is 26,700,000 ev.

Despite this veritable flood of energy evolved by the formation of a single helium atom from hydrogen, it requires the formation of 630,000,000 tons of helium from hydrogen *every second* to keep the Sun radiating.

We might have a moment of alarm that the Sun, expending energy at this fantastic rate, might soon run down by consuming all its hydrogen and running out of fuel. This, however, is not an immediate danger. The Sun has been in existence and shining, according to the best available evidence, for some 6 billion years but even so there is enough hydrogen left in its structure to keep it going at the present rate for at least 8 billion years more without any significant change in its appearance or behavior.

Therefore, we may place the hydrogen-fusion reaction on the extreme left of our energy roller-coaster and forget about it. We may have to worry about replacing the ATP as fast as it is consumed or else it will all be gone in a matter of minutes; and, working backward, we must worry about replacing the glucose as fast as it is consumed or else it will all be gone in a matter of weeks (in an individual human body); but, working backward still farther, we don't have to worry about replacing the solar hydrogen. There is enough and to spare for all the time man can reasonably be expected to look into the future.*

The Sun is the energy-source that not only powers all of life, but powers also most of the non-living energy-sources used by man. Wood, coal, and oil are all the products of past plant life. The power of the wind depends on the Sun's unequal heating of the atmosphere. Water power depends on the Sun's evaporation of vast quantities of sea water and on the upward movement of the vapor for miles. Energy-sources that do *not* depend on the Sun include the tides, the earth's internal heat and, of course, uranium fission plus other man-induced nuclear reactions.

* Nevertheless one might ask, out of curiosity, "But how did the solar hydrogen get there in the first place and what happens when it is all gone?" Such a question is of concern to astronomers and for some details on their thinking in this respect see my book *The Universe* (New York: Walker and Company, 1966).

Particles of Energy

Now that we are satisfied that there is enough solar energy in existence to power the carbon cycle, let us pass on to the question of just how much sunlight is needed for each glucose molecule. But how does one most conveniently measure rays of sunlight?

For an answer, we must go back, to begin with, to 1900, and the work of a German physicist, Max Planck. Thanks to him, the whole question of energy took on a new aspect.

Planck worked out a theory of heat radiation that made it seem that such radiation did *not* stream out of a hot object in the form of a continuous fluid that could be broken up into "drops" of any size however small as had been assumed prior to his time. Rather, heat radiation streamed out in the form of tiny fragments of energy of specific size. It was almost as though energy, like matter, consisted of particles.

These energy particles Planck called "quanta," a word for which "quantum" is the singular. (This is, actually, a Latin word meaning "how much?" because the crucial question concerning the energy particles was their size.)

Planck's view of energy was called the "quantum theory" and, within a very few years, it was found to apply not only to radiant heat but to all forms of energy.

Well, then, how large is a quantum?

In order to give an answer we must first consider the nature of light. Light can most easily be understood as a kind of rapidly pulsating field of electromagnetic force, spreading outward from its source at 186,282 miles per second (in a vacuum). This rapidly pulsating field can be represented as an endless series of waves. The length of an individual wave in such a representation is a "wavelength."

Different wavelength-sizes of light affect our eye differently and this is interpreted by the brain as a variety of colors. What we call red light has a comparatively large wavelength. The various shades of orange light have shorter wavelengths, yellow light still shorter, followed by green, blue, and, finally, violet light. The last has the shortest wavelengths.

This list of colors, from red to violet, includes only "visible light." There are wavelengths longer than those of red light and these do not affect the retina of the eye and are therefore invisible. These include the radiations we speak of as infrared waves, microwaves, and radio waves. Though these cannot be seen they can be detected by appropriate instruments.

Then, too, there are wavelengths shorter than those of violet light and these are also invisible since they do not affect the retina in such a way as to give rise to a sensation of light. (These very short-wave radiations can damage the retina physically, however, and are therefore dangerous; all the more so for being invisible.) Included among the short-wave radiations are ultraviolet waves, x-rays and gamma rays. These, too, can be detected by appropriate instruments.

The entire range of these radiations is referred to as the "electromagnetic spectrum."

The Sun radiates waves representing the entire range of the spectrum, but, as it happens, our atmosphere is transparent only to those sections of the spectrum which include visible light and microwaves. Furthermore, the temperature of the Sun's surface is such that it radiates most intensely in the range of visible light.

As a result, even though visible light makes up only a tiny fraction of the total electromagnetic spectrum, nearly half of all the radiation that reaches the earth's surface from the Sun is visible light. (Our eyes have evolved and adapted themselves to react to this portion of the electromagnetic spectrum because it is the portion that reaches us in the greatest quantity, so it is not really a remarkable coincidence that visible light is so favored. It is because it is so favored that it is visible.)

The wavelengths of visible light are small indeed. Even the deepest red color, just barely visible, representing the longest wavelengths present in visible light, has a wavelength of just 0.00003 inches. The shortest wavelength of violet light are about half as long, or 0.000015 inches.

Another important quantity in connection with electromagnetic radiation is its "frequency"; that is, the number of waves produced in one second.

In one second, light travels 186,282 miles, or about 11,600,-000,000 inches. In that second, enough waves must be formed to fit this huge length. If each wave is 0.00003 inches long, as in the case of extreme red light, then just about 400,000,000,000,000 (four hundred trillion) waves fit into the length. Extreme violet light has waves just half as long as those of extreme red light and therefore twice as many will fit into the distance light covers in one second. In short, the frequency of visible light ranges from 400 trillion at the extreme red to 800 trillion at the extreme violet.

Planck showed that the size of a quantum of energy of electromagnetic radiation is directly proportional to the frequency. Since extreme violet light had twice the frequency of extreme red light, the quanta of extreme violet light were twice as large as the quanta of extreme red light.

Quanta can only be absorbed as wholes. If violet light shines upon matter, the molecules of that matter absorb whole quanta that are twice as large as they would be if that same matter were absorbing quanta of red light.

The larger the individual quanta that are absorbed, the larger the energy supply made available to the molecules and the higher that molecule can be shoved up the energy roller-coaster. It follows, then, that violet light can bring about chemical changes, which red light (with its half-size quanta) cannot. It is for this reason, for instance, that photographic darkrooms can be lit by red light. The small quanta of the red light will not bring about the changes on the film that other colors of light will.

It is for this reason, too, that violet light is said to be "more energetic" than red light. Obviously, strong red light will contain more total energy than a feeble ray of violet light, but the violet light will come in larger pieces, so to speak, and it is the size of the individual piece that counts in bringing about chemical changes, not the number of pieces.

We can see something similar in ordinary affairs, if we consider a large rock which can be lifted by a strong man, but which cannot be budged by a twelve-year-old child. A single man can lift it, but a million children would fail if they tried one after the other. To be sure, three children might lift the rock if they crowded around it and heaved simultaneously and three small quanta might do the work of one large quantum if they happened to strike the molecule at the same time and were simultaneously absorbed. However, simultaneous absorption of quanta is even rarer than cooperation among children.

Planck was able to show exactly how to determine the size of the quantum. The frequency had to be multiplied by a certain fixed number which physicists were soon to call "Planck's constant" in his honor.

The size of the quantum is represented by e and Planck's constant by h. The frequency is represented by the Greek letter "nu" which is written ν. Planck's equation is therefore $e = h\nu$. This is more famous to physicists of the twentieth century than any other equation, with the exception of Einstein's $e = mc^2$.

The value of the frequency of visible light is very large, of course—in the hundreds of trillions. One might think that if such a huge number were multiplied by h, it would be bound to give a huge answer and that the size of the quantum would prove enormous.

That, however, depends on the size of h. If h were sufficiently tiny, it would reduce even a number like 800 trillion to minute dimensions. It turns out that the value of h is extremely tiny indeed; tiny enough to much more than make up for the high frequency.

The value of h, as given most frequently in reference books, is 0.00000000000000000000000000066256 erg-seconds. If the frequency of light is multiplied by this number, however, we would get the size of the quantum in ergs. This is not what we want, for in this book, we have been using electron-volts (ev) as the unit of energy.

To get the value of the size of the quantum in ev, we must use a different expression: $h = 0.00000000000000413$ ev-seconds. Using this expression, it turns out that the size of the least energetic quantum of visible light (extreme red) is equal to 1.65 ev.

The size of the most energetic quantum of visible light (extreme violet) is just twice as great, since the frequency is twice as great. It is 3.3 ev.

With our mind on light in terms of quanta, let's turn once more to the carbon cycle. Chlorophyll, the key compound in photosynthesis, strongly absorbs red light and violet light, but reflects most of the light at intermediate wavelengths. The mixture of colors in the reflected light appears green to the eye, which is exactly why vegetation is that color.*

Only light that is absorbed can affect chemical reactions and it follows that red light or violet light or both can supply the energy for photosynthesis. As it happens, even the less energetic red light can do so easily and photosynthesis proceeds with ease in the presence of red light that is 0.000026 inches in wavelength and that has a frequency of 450 trillion. Such light has quanta that are 1.85 ev in size.

It would take 16 quanta of this size, working at 100 per cent efficiency, to form one molecule of glucose out of carbon dioxide and water. While biochemists still argue on the actual efficiency of the photosynthetic process, a good estimate seems to be that under favorable conditions it can be no more than 30 per cent efficient. (Under unfavorable conditions it may be only 3 per cent efficient.) Assuming the favorable conditions, we can say that 54 quanta of red light (just about 100 ev) will produce a molecule of glucose. (Some say only 48 quanta are necessary.)

This gives us a new version of the energy roller-coaster, one that begins with solar energy (see Figure 24).

If we reduce matters to a single carbon atom (a sixth-glucose)

* Charles Erwin Wilson, the General Motors official who was America's Secretary of Defense from 1953 to 1957, once indulged himself in a sneer at research scientists. He spoke of them as people who weren't interested in practical problems but were interested instead in far-out questions such as why the grass is green. One can scarcely imagine a more ignorant remark or see more clearly the follies of what is usually called "being practical." To find out why the grass is green is to understand how chlorophyll works and to understand that is to have knowledge concerning one of the basic chemical reactions that makes all life possible. If mankind could learn to manipulate that reaction to his advantage it might utterly dwarf the achievements of every "practical man" who ever worked at General Motors.

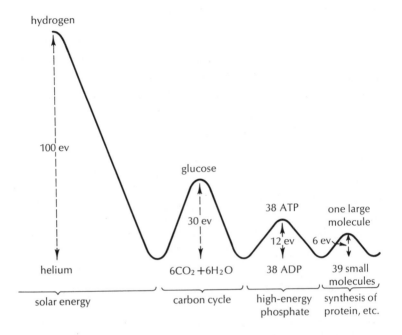

Figure 24. The Energy Roller-coaster (with Solar Energy)

rather than an entire glucose molecule, we can once again present the carbon cycle, this time with the roller-coaster beginning with solar energy on the left (see Figure 25). There are nine quanta (possibly only eight) utilized per sixth-glucose.

On a Planetary Scale

Now let's return to the total energy of sunlight. This was brought up at the very beginning of the chapter to demonstrate that there was enough energy in sunlight to run the carbon cycle. With the energy details of light worked out, let's take up the matter again and see if we can't extract some interesting information as far as the earth is concerned and the life upon it.

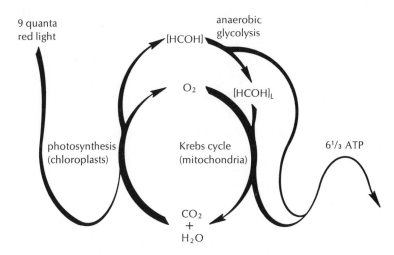

Figure 25. The Carbon Cycle (with Quanta)

Altogether, about 1,250,000,000,000,000,000,000 kilocalories of solar energy strike the Earth every year as it circles smoothly in its orbit. Of this about 60 per cent is reflected by Earth's clouds or is absorbed by various gases and particles in Earth's atmosphere. This means that 40 per cent, or about 500,000,000,000,-000,000,000 kilocalories, reaches the Earth's surface each year.

Of this energy, fully one-half is in the infra-red region, where the quanta are too feeble to be of any use in photosynthesis, which means that 250,000,000,000,000,000,000 kilocalories of sufficiently energetic quanta reach the Earth's surface each year. Some 40 per cent of this is likely to be reflected by the ocean surface, by rocks and sand, or even by plant life itself, so that only 60 per cent is actually absorbed by the plant life on land and sea.

This brings us down to 150,000,000,000,000,000,000 kilocalories of solar energy per year actually absorbed by the plants, and potentially capable of being put to use in photosynthesis.

Let us divide this, as a rough guess, into half in the red-orange region and half in the blue-violet region—75,000,000,000,000,-000,000 kilocalories per year in each region.

To make the number more manageable, let us calculate it per second. The plants of the world, both on land and sea, absorb 2,400,000,000,000 kilocalories of red-orange light, and the same quantity of blue-violet light each second. Let us simplify matters by supposing that the red-orange light is composed entirely of quanta of 1.8 ev each while the blue-violet light is composed of quanta of 3.6 ev each.

Since each kilocalorie is equal to 23,000,000,000,000,000,-000,000 ev, we can calculate that the total number of quanta absorbed by plant life each second is of the order of 45,000,000,-000,000,000,000,000,000,000,000,000.

Allowing 54 quanta to form one molecule of glucose out of carbon dioxide and water, then each second sees something like 800,000,000,000,000,000,000,000,000,000,000,000 molecules of glucose formed. (That's 800 million trillion trillion molecules.)

An individual glucose molecule is tiny, but 800 million trillion trillion of them mount up. That number of molecules represents the formation of the equivalent of 260,000 tons of glucose each second.

How does this compare with the quantity of glucose that could be formed if all the Sun's energy, without exception, were used for the purpose with perfect efficiency? Earlier in the chapter, I had estimated this to be 215,000,000,000 tons in ten hours, which is equivalent to 6,000,000 tons per second. This we might call the "ideal maximum."

It's not surprising that the ideal maximum can't be reached. So much of the Sun's radiation is lost by reflection and so much of the remainder is useless infra-red, that we must expect there is a "practical maximum" that is much smaller than the ideal maximum. It is this practical maximum I have calculated after allowing for losses of all sorts, and it comes to 260,000 tons per second which is only 5 per cent of the ideal maximum.

Even that is too good, for in actual practice, the earth's plant life falls far short of producing even the practical maximum of glucose.

How much is actually formed by plant life? One reasonable

estimate is about 400,000,000,000 tons per year. This is equivalent to 12,500 tons of glucose formed per second, which is only 5 per cent of the practical maximum and only 0.25 per cent of the ideal maximum.

Why do plants fall so far short of even the practical maximum? For one thing, the figure of 54 quanta per molecule of glucose (representing 30 per cent efficiency) is attained only under favorable circumstances. Under actual circumstances, the efficiency is likely to be as little as 3 per cent and not 54 but 540 quanta are required. Right there the quantity of glucose formed is cut to a tenth the practical maximum.

Then, too, sunlight is not always the bottleneck. The fertility of the soil and the water supply are two other important considerations. In dry soil and barren soil no quantity of sunlight is going to produce much glucose, for growing plants will be few and far between if present at all.

But let's do some more calculating.

If the plant life of the world produces some 400,000,000,000 tons of glucose each year, then that quantity of glucose or its equivalent, but no more, can be eaten (or decomposed by bacteria) each year without reducing the total quantity of plant life on Earth. The quantity of kilocalories in that tonnage is 1,500,000,-000,000,000,000.

To support a human being reasonably requires a little over 2,000 kilocalories per day, or just about 750,000 kilocalories per year. If, then, all the plant growth in the world were invested in human beings *only* (meaning that all other competing animal life on land and sea, from whales to aphids, were ruthlessly eliminated) our planet would be able to support a population of some 2,000,000,000,000,000 (two trillion). This is six hundred times Earth's present population of 3,300,000,000.

However, at the present rate of increase of mankind (with the earth's population doubling every fifty years) our planet will contain two trillion human beings by 2450.

In other words, if mankind does not find some way of limiting his own multiplication then he will have reached the limit to which he can increase his food supply (under present conditions) in less than 500 years.

And in order to reach a population of two trillion and support it, mankind will have to kill off all other animal life and live on a purely vegetarian diet. Conservationists and all who are interested in the animal life of this planet should be aware of this. The very first order of business for any sincere conservationist is to drive for human population control.

It is, of course, quite uncertain that mankind can kill off all animal life, even if he should want to, and a world free of animals might be an ecologically impossible one for man to live in. It is certain therefore that long before 2450 A.D. is reached, man's population will be balanced, if not by a lower birth-rate then by a higher death-rate.

Of course, there are some who are invincibly optimistic about the possible advances of science. Suppose animal life can be killed off without harm to humanity, and suppose land and sea are fertilized and watered to the point where the practical maximum of glucose production is obtained.

Suppose that we go farther still and manage to trap the sunlight that is reflected by Earth's clouds and surface, and manage to bend infra-red light to photosynthetic purposes, and manage to use light at 100 per cent efficiency. Suppose, in short, that we achieve what would seem to be the impossible, and reach the ideal maximum of glucose production; the quantity obtained when every ray of sunlight is reached. That will allow food production to be raised to 400 times that which now prevails and make possible, in theory, a population of 800,000,000,000,000.

But if Earth's population were to continue to increase unchecked, then by 2800, the number of people on earth would have reached the 800 trillion figure and there would no longer be sufficient energy in all the sunlight we get to support any further increase by the ordinary process of photosynthesis.

I am deliberately not considering the impossible burden of catastrophe that the population increase would bring upon us long before so ridiculous a figure as 800 trillion is reached. I am not considering the destruction of resources, the increase of pollution, the difficulties of distribution, the loss of space and privacy, the increasing tensions. Let us say that all such problems can somehow be handled and solved.

Even so, the race, at the present level of multiplication, will outrun the Sun itself in considerably less than a thousand years, and that is the most dramatic way I know of to indicate the seriousness of the present "population explosion."*

---

* To carry matters to a completely ridiculous extreme, we can say this. If it were conceivable that mankind could multiply at its present rate till 5200 A.D. the total mass of humanity would then equal that of the Sun. If they continued till 9000 A.D. the total mass of humanity would equal that of the known universe. Obviously, even if every star in the universe had Earth-like planets and if we could colonize them all as freely and as quickly as we chose, we still couldn't continue our present increase for more than a couple of thousand years.

6

Isotopes and the Cycle

Carbon Dioxide or Water

We are left now with the necessity of describing the details of the upward half of the cycle—photosynthesis—as we have already done in the case of the downward half.

Photosynthesis was the harder portion of the cycle to solve, partly because of a physical hurdle, but even more so because of a psychological one.

Physically, sunlight is involved in photosynthesis and it is not easy to work with something as subtle as sunlight. A green leaf is exposed to sunlight and carbon dioxide and water are converted to tissue substances in a matter of seconds. What has happened in that brief interval and, most of all, what is it—in detail—that the sunlight has done? It is only in the course of this last generation that biologists have had the techniques to handle brief bursts of light and the effects they bring about.

The psychological difficulty was this: Most biologists who worked with photosynthesis before the 1930's thought they knew what sunlight did in general terms, if not in detail—but they were wrong!

We can see, perhaps, why they got onto the wrong track. In respiration, glucose combines with oxygen to form carbon dioxide and water. The glucose itself, however, already has some oxygen in it, and that was a misleading factor.

If we consider the familiar equation of glucose oxidation, it is not easy to see that, but let's rewrite it making use of a slightly modified formula for glucose. Instead of writing glucose as

$C_6H_{12}O_6$, let's write it $C_6(H_2O)_6$, as though there were a string of six carbon atoms with each carbon atom attached to a water molecule. This makes the total number of each kind of atom come out correctly, but it is a wrong (WRONG) conception of the *structure* of the glucose molecule (see page 39). Nevertheless, let's write the equation for glucose oxidation by making use of this wrong formula for glucose:

$$C_6(H_2O)_6 + 6O_2 \longrightarrow 6CO_2 + 6H_2O$$

(Equation 27)

If we look at Equation 27, it is almost inevitable that we would think, somehow, that the water molecules fell off the carbon chain, so to speak, and that the naked carbon atoms then combined with oxygen to form carbon dioxide. In other words, the oxygen atoms that were in the air to begin with, end up in carbon dioxide molecules.

Even after the true structure of glucose and similar compounds was worked out, beginning in the 1870's, and it was known that no intact water groups were present in the glucose molecule, old habits of thought persisted.

What's more, it even seemed like "common sense." (It is impossible to be too firm in the assurance that "common sense" is a dangerous guide in science.) People (even biologists) have automatically thought that oxygen was the "good air" we breathed in and carbon dioxide was the "bad air" we breathed out and that, therefore, the oxygen was just naturally converted into carbon dioxide.

The water vapor that appears in expired breath tended to be ignored. It was easy to assume that the air just picked it up from the moist inner surface of the lungs. Even when chemists realized that water molecules were formed in the course of glucose oxidation, they were still not impressed. Water seemed to be merely the "background" of life, rather than an active participant.

We can argue, then, that since photosynthesis is the opposite of respiration, and since in respiration oxygen is converted to carbon dioxide, it follows that in photosynthesis carbon dioxide is reconverted into oxygen.

Probably almost every biochemist and biologist before the 1930's would have accepted the following (WRONG) statements as very likely true:

The action of sunlight is to break up the carbon dioxide molecule and two general results followed: 1) the oxygen is liberated into the atmosphere (oxygen formation), and 2) the carbon is combined with other atoms and converted into tissue constituents (carbon fixation—so-called, because carbon was transferred from a free, gaseous molecule to fixed, solid ones).

By this view it would seem that oxygen formation and carbon fixation were parts of the same process and could not be separated.

Slowly, however, a minority view began to obtrude itself. In the 1910's and 1920's, it became more and more apparent that the energy produced in respiration arose through the union of atmospheric oxygen with the *hydrogen* of foodstuffs to produce water. The carbon dioxide produced by respiration did not result from any direct combination of carbon and atmospheric oxygen but arose through decarboxylation (see page 101).

Might not one argue that since energy arose from the combination of hydrogen and oxygen to form water, energy was required to split water into hydrogen and oxygen? In other words, photosynthesis reversed respiration by splitting water, rather than splitting carbon dioxide.

Maybe so, but the difficulty with such an argument is that we can't be sure we are justified in supposing that photosynthesis is the complete opposite of respiration. It is the overall opposite but it may not be the opposite in every last detail. That is, you may drive from Chicago to New York and then from New York back to Chicago, but surely it is possible that you may follow two different routes in doing so.

So we can't really argue by opposites to show that sunlight splits either carbon dioxide or water. The situation is uncertain, at least from this standpoint.

As more was learned about the chemical machinery of cells, though, it was discovered that carbon dioxide was fixed by a number of processes in any cell, whether photosynthetic or not. In non-photosynthetic cells carbon dioxide fixation was never a major process while in photosynthetic cells it was, but suppose one made comparisons anyway.

In all the various chemical mechanisms that fixed carbon dioxide in non-photosynthetic cells, oxygen was never produced. This meant that carbon dioxide fixation and oxygen formation were not necessarily part of the same process. Perhaps they were not part of the same process in photosynthetic cells either and in that case, the oxygen formed had to come from water.

Unfortunately, this second point was unconvincing, too. Photosynthetic cells make use of sunlight in the course of carbon dioxide fixation, and non-photosynthetic cells do not, and that is a huge difference. It may be that chemical reactions go on in the presence of sunlight that do not go on in its absence. It is difficult, therefore, to argue convincingly that what happens in a non-photosynthetic cell can be a guide to what goes on in a photosynthetic one.

In 1937, something still more pertinent occurred. An English biochemist, Robert Hill, developed a technique for mashing up green leaves that broke up the cells but left the chloroplasts apparently intact. Actually, though, the chloroplasts were not intact. They had suffered some sort of damage because they could no longer bring about photosynthesis. Apparently, some component or components of the complex enzyme system within the chloroplast had leaked away and would have to be replaced before anything could be accomplished.

One of the processes that goes on universally in cells is the transfer of hydrogen atoms from one substance to another. (This happens in the cytochrome system, for instance—see page 103.) As one way of trying to substitute for some missing substance, Hill added certain iron compounds which he knew were capable of accepting hydrogen atoms. If some natural hydrogen-acceptor or acceptors had vanished from the chloroplast, the iron compounds might substitute.

The iron compounds *did* substitute. When the damaged chloroplasts were exposed to light in the presence of the iron compounds, oxygen began to form at a brisk rate. Carbon fixation, on the other hand, did not occur.

The "Hill reaction," as it was called, showed that oxygen formation and carbon dioxide fixation were not necessarily part of the same process even in photosynthetic cells. One could go on while the other did not. This meant that the oxygen had to be produced from the water molecule. In favor of this notion was the efficacy of the iron compounds. Light could not break down the water molecule in quantity and form oxygen unless (so it would seem) some mechanism existed to carry off the hydrogen. The fact that hydrogen transfer and oxygen formation went together argued in favor of the breakdown of water as the prime action of sunlight.

Yet even this was not foolproof. Hill was working with damaged chloroplasts and with non-natural hydrogen acceptors. Could he be certain that he was studying the actual process as it would go on in intact chloroplasts with natural hydrogen acceptors?

Although the evidence in favor of water as the source for the oxygen was slowly piling up, it remained inconclusive.

For a conclusive test, what one really needed was a method for marking oxygen atoms. If one could, for instance, use carbon dioxide with one kind of oxygen atoms ("oxygen A") and water with another kind ("oxygen B"), a photosynthesizing cell could be exposed to both and the oxygen produced could be tested. If the oxygen produced were "oxygen A" it would have originated from carbon dioxide and if it were "oxygen B" it could have originated from water.

But how can one go about marking oxygen atoms?

Marking the Oxygen Atoms

Throughout the nineteenth century, the notion of marking oxygen atoms so as to tell one from another would have seemed mere fantasy. Chemists were then firmly convinced (on the basis of all available evidence) that all atoms of any given element were absolutely identical and that no way existed of distinguishing one from another.

In the last decade of the nineteenth century, however, radioactivity was discovered and this presented chemists with a completely new set of observations that gave them a much deeper insight into the structure within the atom.

It was discovered that atoms were not featureless spheres but had an intricate internal structure. Each atom had most of its mass concentrated in a very tiny structure—the atomic nucleus— at the very center of the atom. The nucleus, it was eventually discovered, was made up of two kinds of particles: Protons and neutrons. They were rather similar in many ways, but the protons carried a positive electric charge while the neutrons were electrically neutral.

All atoms of a particular element had the same number of protons in their nuclei. They did not, however, necessarily all have the same number of neutrons. This meant that some atoms of an element could be distinguished from others by means of the differing number of their neutrons.

Protons and neutrons are just about equal in mass. It is customary to set the mass of protons and of neutrons arbitrarily equal to 1, for simplicity's sake. In order to get the mass of a particular atomic nucleus, it is therefore only necessary to count the total number of protons and neutrons that the nucleus contains.

As an example, let us consider the atoms of the element neon. (I choose neon because it was the first non-radioactive element in which the presence of slightly different atoms was recognized. This was in 1912.)

All neon atoms have nuclei containing 10 protons. Out of every 1,000 neon atoms, however, 909 have 10 neutrons, 88 have 12 neutrons and 3 have 11 neutrons.

If we consider protons and neutrons as having unit mass, then the mass of the neon atom with 10 protons and 10 neutrons in its nucleus is 20. The other two varieties have masses of 22 and 21 respectively. We can identify the three varieties of neon as "neon-20," "neon-22" and "neon-21." In symbols, we can say ^{20}Ne, ^{22}Ne, and ^{21}Ne. Such atomic varieties, differing only in neutron content, are called "isotopes." Neon, as it is found in nature, is made up of three isotopes.

The various isotopes of an element have virtually identical chemical properties and are very difficult to separate by the ordinary methods of the chemical laboratory. The earliest way of distinguishing between isotopes clearly was to subject atoms such as those of neon to a magnetic field while in flight.

Under the circumstances chosen, the neon atoms would curve in their flight in response to the field; but the more massive atoms, being more sluggish, would curve the least. At the conclusion of the curve, the neon atoms would end on a photographic plate and make their mark there. Each isotope, having curved to a different extent, would end in a slightly different position and, from that position, the extent of curvature of its path and, therefore, its mass, could be calculated. An instrument which distinguishes and measures the mass of the isotopes of an element in this way is called a "mass spectrograph."

As the years passed, it was found that not neon only but most elements consisted of two or more isotopes. In 1929, two American chemists, William Francis Giauque and H. L. Johnson, were able to show that oxygen consisted of 3 isotopes. By far the most common variety of the oxygen atom contained 8 protons and 8 neutrons in its nucleus and was "oxygen-16." Out of every 10,000 oxygen atoms, no less than 9,976 are oxygen-16. Of the remaining 24 atoms, however, 20 are oxygen-18 (8 protons and 10 neutrons) and 4 are oxygen-17 (8 protons and 9 neutrons).

The existence of isotopes makes it possible to mark atoms.

Suppose a plant is exposed to carbon dioxide containing oxygen atoms in the usual mixture of oxygens (almost entirely oxygen-16) and to water containing an unusually large percentage of oxygen-18. It is only necessary then to test the evolved oxygen to see if it contains a large percentage of oxygen-18 or not. If it does, that oxygen-18 could have come only from the water. Oxygen-18 is used here as a "tracer" (for it traces the course of a reaction, so to speak).

It is not easy to obtain water with oxygen-18 in high concentration, but it can be done. One way is to electrolyze water, that is, to split it into hydrogen and oxygen by means of an electric current. The more massive molecules are less readily split. This means that as more and more water molecules are electrolyzed, the liquid water that remains becomes richer and richer in those molecules containing oxygen-17 and oxygen-18. Eventually, it is possible to obtain samples of water in which 10 per cent of the oxygen atoms (rather than 0.02 per cent) are oxygen-18.

In 1941, a group of American chemists led by S. Ruben and M. Kamen exposed photosynthesizing cells to water enriched in oxygen-18. The oxygen evolved by such cells contained oxygen-18 in the exact amount one would expect if it were derived entirely from the water.

One might still argue that water and carbon dioxide might "equilibrate"; that is, rapidly exchange oxygen atoms so that both would end up with a roughly equal share of the oxygen-18. In that case the evolved oxygen might come from both water and carbon dioxide. However, careful tests in which carbon dioxide and isotope-enriched water were mixed and studied showed that equilibration did not take place.

That settled the matter, then. It is now generally accepted that the energy supplied by sunlight serves to split the water molecule. The hydrogen atoms produced are taken up by certain hydrogen acceptors and eventually are added to carbon dioxide molecules to form glucose and tissue components generally. The oxygen atoms produced in this way find themselves in the atmosphere as molecular oxygen.

The Pathway of Water

To form a molecule of oxygen, two molecules of water have to be split apart, so that four hydrogen atoms are formed. This is an "uphill reaction," energetically speaking, and quanta of sunlight must be supplied. The four hydrogen atoms will eventually (as we shall see) react with a molecule of carbon dioxide to form a sixth-glucose; so this means that nine (or possibly eight) quanta are required (see page 122). We can therefore write this particular reaction as:

$$2H_2O + 8 \text{ or } 9 \text{ quanta} \longrightarrow 4[H] + O_2$$

(Equation 28)

(I write the hydrogen in brackets to show that it is not set free in molecular form as oxygen is, but is transferred to a hydrogen acceptor.)

Where does chlorophyll fit in here? Why can't the quanta do the job by themselves? They have the energy for it. In short, why can't we expose water to sunlight and have the water molecules break up? The water molecules can indeed absorb quanta of sunlight and become "activated"; that is, assume a higher-energy structure. This higher-energy structure might break apart, but it is apparently much more likely that the energy is simply given off again immediately, as energy, and the atoms of the water molecule continue to hang together.

If you look back at Figure 10 on page 51 at the structural formula of chlorophyll, however, you will see that it is made up of numerous single and double bonds in alternation. Such an alternating system is particularly stable. When chlorophyll absorbs light and is activated, instead of giving up the energy again almost at once, it hangs on to the energy for a perceptible time, for activated chlorophyll (thanks to its single-double alternation of bonds) is more stable than activated water would be. Perhaps, as the energy lingers on in the activated chlorophyll molecule, there is time to transfer that energy to water in a way that enables the hydrogen and oxygen atoms to be separated.

I say "perhaps" because although the notion just advanced may sound good, it doesn't work. If chlorophyll (taken by itself and not as part of a chloroplast) is mixed with water and exposed to light, no oxygen is formed even if a hydrogen acceptor is added.

The beginning of an answer to this puzzle came in 1932, when two American biochemists, R. Emerson and W. Arnold, illuminated plant cells with very short flashes of light, each a ten-thousandth of a second in duration, separated by dark periods of a thousandth of a second each. The dark period was long enough for the chlorophyll molecules to give up all the energy they had gained in the previous flash of light and to drop from activated chlorophyll to ground-level chlorophyll, so to speak. With each new flash of light, the chlorophyll started from scratch.

During the flash of light, the chlorophyll molecules were activated and split water molecules, forming molecular oxygen. If the intensity of the flash of light were increased, more chlorophyll molecules snatched at quanta, more were activated, more water molecules were split, more oxygen molecules were formed.

Eventually, at a certain intensity of light, the quantity of oxygen evolved during the flash reached a maximum. Making the flash even brighter did not help. Emerson and Arnold decided that what had happened at that point was that every chlorophyll molecule was at work and nothing more could be done by adding still more light. (You can't pour more water into a full glass.)

Emerson and Arnold calculated how many quanta had been absorbed by the chlorophyll molecules when those molecules were working at maximum speed. They would not have been surprised if it had turned out that each separate chlorophyll molecule had absorbed one quantum of red light.

But that was not so. It turned out that only one quantum of red light was absorbed for every 250 molecules of chlorophyll present. In later years, when the chloroplasts were examined in detail by the electron microscope, it turned out that they contained small flattened discs of chlorophyll, each disc containing about 250 closely-stacked molecules of chlorophyll.

The porphyrin ring of the chlorophyll is flat so the stacking can be close indeed, like a series of poker chips. And what keeps them that way? One very plausible suggestion involves the long phytyl chain attached to one corner of the porphyrin right (see page 51). The phytyl chain mixes easily with fatty molecules of the type present in the chloroplast membrane. These chains are buried in the membrane, like so many lollipop sticks, holding the porphyrin rings in tight flat-to-flat contact.

It is as though 250 porphyrin rings were kept close enough together to form what amounts to a single molecule with 250 times as many single-double bond alternations as in a single porphyrin ring. A quantum of light can enter the stack at some sensitive point and then distribute its energy over a much larger and much more stable multiple-molecule, and that energy can then be used to break the water molecule.

This would explain why water is split when intact chloroplasts with their chlorophyll-stacks, are used, but not when separate and independent chlorophyll molecules are present in ordinary solution.

The hydrogen atoms produced from the water molecules are transferred to an acceptor and then passed on from molecule to molecule—perhaps by way of several varieties of chlorophyll. We might talk here of a "chlorophyll system" with hydrogen passed along it, just as in the case of the Krebs cycle, where we had a cytochrome system (see page 103).

ATP is produced at several points in the cytochrome system and it is also produced at several points in the chlorophyll system. The actual process by which ATP is formed at specific points is, as yet, equally obscure in both cases.

In the cytochrome system the hydrogen atoms are eventually added to oxygen to form water. It is this combination that ultimately supplies the energy for ATP formation so that the process is called oxidative phosphorylation.

In the chlorophyll system the hydrogen atoms need not, and do not, combine with oxygen. The energy for ATP formation comes from sunlight and the process is therefore called "photophosphorylation." With energy coming from sunlight and not from hydrogen-oxygen combination, the hydrogen atoms produced by the photosynthetic splitting of water can take part in an "uphill," energy-consuming reaction at the expense of the "light-formed" ATP—and they do. The hydrogen atoms combine with carbon dioxide to form glucose, thus:

$$4[H] + CO_2 \longrightarrow [HCOH] + H_2O$$

(Equation 29)

Suppose we consider Equations 28 and 29 together. The four hydrogen atoms that are formed by the break up of water are consumed by the carbon dioxide molecule, and can be cancelled out. Ignoring the energy aspects—the quanta of light and the ATP molecules—we have:

$$2H_2O + CO_2 \longrightarrow [HCOH] + H_2O + O_2$$

(Equation 30)

If you look at Equations 28 and 29 carefully and see how they combine to form Equation 30, you will see that the oxygen molecule on the right in Equation 30 comes entirely from the two water molecules on the left. One of the two atoms of oxygen in the carbon dioxide molecule on the left of Equation 30 goes into the sixth-glucose on the right; the other goes into the water molecule on the right.

To be sure, the water molecule on the right may be split at a later stage and its oxygen atom eventually may contribute to the formation of molecular oxygen in the atmosphere. In this way, the oxygen of the atmosphere may arise out of carbon dioxide but—insofar as it is produced by photosynthesis—never directly.

The direct source of the oxygen of the atmosphere is water. If the oxygen arises ultimately from carbon dioxide, that is only because that carbon dioxide must first contribute its oxygen to the formation of a water molecule.

If we were to deal with Equation 30 without the information given us by the use of oxygen-18, we might decide that water molecules are, after all, merely water molecules. If two are on the left side of Equation 30 and one on the right side, we could simplify matters by "cancelling" a water molecule on each side, writing:

$$H_2O + CO_2 \longrightarrow [HCOH] + O_2$$

(Equation 31)

This obscures the fact, however, that oxygen arises from the water molecule, for in Equation 31, there just isn't enough oxygen in water for the purpose. There is only one oxygen atom in the water molecule and there are two in the oxygen molecule, so that we would be forced to conclude (WRONGLY!) that at least one of the oxygen atoms in the oxygen molecule must be derived from carbon dioxide.

Oxygen-18 experiments show us this is wrong and we must therefore make use of Equation 30 and not Equation 31. In fact, we can make matters clearer by distinguishing between the oxygen atoms originally in water and those originally in carbon dioxide by writing the latter as O*. Now we can rewrite Equation 30 as:

$$2H_2O + CO^*_2 \longrightarrow [HCO^*H] + H_2O^* + O_2$$

(Equation 32)

With all this in mind, we can prepare a new version of the carbon cycle as in Figure 26, omitting the roller-coaster aspect since that may now be taken for granted.

Notice how this new diagram shows the points I have tried to make in this section. The oxidation of a sixth-glucose by a molecule of oxygen forms only a single water molecule, but two must

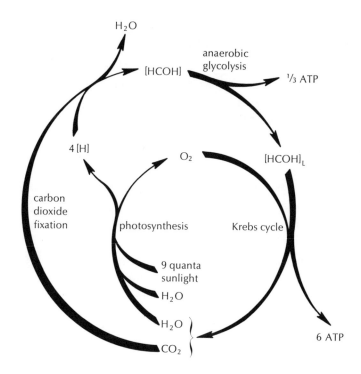

Figure 26. The Carbon Cycle (with the Pathway of Water)

be broken up to re-form the oxygen molecule. However, a new water molecule is also formed (making use of an oxygen atom from carbon dioxide) so that with an extra water molecule in and an extra water molecule out, all remains in balance.

Exploding Atoms

A quarter century has passed since tracer experiments have shown that the oxygen produced in photosynthesis comes from the water molecules, but nothing more about the details of the process has been learned.

Unfortunately, while scientists must admit their debt of gratitude to oxygen-18, they must also admit it has its deficiencies. The detection and measurement of oxygen-18 is a tedious and slow process. The slowness isn't fatal in the case of substances entering the photosynthetic mechanism (like water) and substances emerging from it (like oxygen). These are reasonably permanent and can wait for analysis.

But what about chemical intermediates in the water-to-oxygen process? What about substances that form and are consumed very quickly in the middle of the process? How can one snatch out these substances and make them sit still while their oxygen-18 content is slowly determined? Unfortunately, this cannot be done.

And yet there are certain isotopes which can be detected and measured with great ease and quickness, even when present in the merest trifling amounts.

The history of such isotopes goes back to 1896 when the phenomenon of radioactivity was first discovered. Scientists came to realize by that discovery (very much to their own astonishment) that some atoms occasionally exploded. Tiny particles were, in the process, hurled out of the atomic nucleus with such energy that they could easily be detected. Even single particles, the product of the explosion of a single atom, could be detected.

What's more, every different kind of exploding atom produced its own types of particles with a characteristic energy content and emerging in characteristic quantities. By studying the nature of the particles detected, it was easy to determine what particular kind of atom was exploding.

At first, the only exploding atoms known were very complex ones like uranium-238 (with a nucleus containing 92 protons and 146 neutrons). These were, for the most part, rare and, without exception, played no role in living processes.

However, the particles produced by radioactive elements served as extremely energetic "bullets" which could be aimed at the nuclei of non-radioactive or "stable atoms." Occasionally, these particles struck a stable nucleus and induced changes in the arrangement of particles within that nucleus. A new atom could be formed, one which might not be present in nature.

This was first accomplished in 1934, by a husband-and-wife

team of French scientists, Frédéric and Irène Joliot-Curie. (She was a daughter of the famous Madame Marie Curie.)

The Joliot-Curies had succeeded in producing a new kind of phosphorus atom. In nature, there appears to be only one kind, with nuclei made up of 15 protons and 16 neutrons so that it is "phosphorus-31." The Joliot-Curies had produced one with 15 protons and 15 neutrons. It was "phosphorus-30."

There was an extremely important difference between phosphorus-31 and phosphorus-30. Phosphorus-31, the naturally-occurring atom, was perfectly stable. Each such atom existed and kept on existing indefinitely. Phosphorus-30, which did not exist in nature, was radioactive. An atom of phosphorus-30 existed for a short time and then exploded, emitting an energetic particle from its nucleus and being converted into another kind of atom (silicon-30) which is stable.

It was this tendency to explode after a short existence that kept phosphorus-30 from existing in nature, so that it was not known to chemists until small quantities were formed by the Joliot-Curies. They received the 1935 Nobel Prize in chemistry for their feat. They had produced the first artificial (man-made, that is) "radioactive isotope."

Naturally, the search was on at once for other radioactive isotopes and it was found that they could be formed easily enough. Radioactive isotopes of element after element were produced. It was not long before they were discovered for every known element without exception.

An exciting vision at once sprang up before the eyes of biochemists. Suppose organic compounds, of the type taking part in the chemical mechanisms within living tissue, were prepared with a radioactive isotope in place of a stable one of the same element. It would be a tracer, indeed. It would require no complicated and expensive mass spectrograph for its slow and uncertain determination. It would, instead, leave a clearly followed track by its own constant explosions.

Detecting devices that pick up the energetic particles produced by exploding radioactive isotopes are quite cheap, accurate and easy to use. Radioactive isotopes can be followed in even the tiniest traces so quickly that for the first time there was hope that isotopes could be used to study not only the input and output compounds of complicated chemical mechanisms like photosynthesis, but the very short-lived intermediate compounds as well.

There were drawbacks, of course; there are always drawbacks.

At first, radioactive isotopes were very expensive and were rather dangerous to handle, too. (The particles and radiations given off by radioactive compounds can disrupt chemical mechanisms within tissue and, in case of excessive exposure, can cause sickness or even death.)

However, during World War II, the research that led to the development of the atomic bomb also led to devices for the production of radioactive isotopes in quantity. By the late 1940's, almost any type of radioactive isotope could be obtained quite cheaply and in sufficient quantities to conduct all the research experiments desired.

Furthermore, atomic bomb research during World War II had led to much knowledge concerning the dangers of radioactive radiations and to the development of effective precautions against those dangers. Post-war scientists, behaving in a careful and rational manner, could work with radioactive substances in all safety.

There remained, however, the radioactive isotopes themselves. Every element had its radioactive isotopes but not every element had suitable ones.

Consider, for instance, the two elements involved in the splitting of water: hydrogen and oxygen.

Hydrogen has two stable isotopes. The more common one has an atomic nucleus made up of a single proton and nothing more; it is hydrogen-1. In 1932, however, the American chemist Harold Clayton Urey was able to detect the presence of minor quantities of a hydrogen isotope with nuclei containing one proton and one neutron. It was hydrogen-2. Out of every 100,000 hydrogen atoms, 15 are hydrogen-2. For this discovery Urey was awarded the Nobel Prize in chemistry for 1934.

Of all the non-radioactive isotopes, hydrogen-2 is the easiest to work with. With a mass of 2, it is fully twice as massive as the common hydrogen-1. No stable isotopes of any other element are so widely different in mass; no other pair has a 100 per cent difference. The greater the difference in mass between the tracer and the common isotope of a given element, the easier and speedier the methods of detection. It follows that in the case of hydrogen, non-radioactive tracer methods are particularly convenient. It is this unusually great difference between hydrogen-2 and hydrogen-1 that led to the former being given a special name of its own, "deuterium" (from a Greek word meaning "second").

In 1939, still a third hydrogen isotope was discovered; one with a nucleus containing one proton and two neutrons. This one, hydrogen-3 (or "tritium," from a Greek word meaning "third") is radioactive. It is the only known radioactive hydrogen isotope.

Tritium can be used in tracer experiments, but it has the difficulty of producing the least energetic explosions of all known artificial radioisotopes. This makes it harder to work with than is ordinarily expected for such substances.

Still with two hydrogen isotopes, the stable deuterium and radioactive tritium, should not something be found out about the inner details of the water pathway in photosynthesis?

Unfortunately not. Hydrogen, being the lightest of all atoms, is the most mobile as well. Hydrogen atoms, more than any others, have the tendency to jump from one molecule to another. A hydrogen atom in one molecule will readily change places with a hydrogen atom in another.

But if a tracer changes places with a normal atom, it becomes useless. The whole value of a tracer is that it is supposed to sit firmly in place and mark the presence of a particular molecule and of other molecules arising from it.

Hydrogen isotopes are particularly useless in this respect, when attached to oxygen atoms, as in water or in glucose. For that reason, neither deuterium nor tritium has been of much help in working out the details of the water pathway.

Suppose we pass on to oxygen. As I said earlier, oxygen atoms come in three stable isotopes: oxygen-16, oxygen-17, and oxygen-

18. Oxygen-18 has been useful, within limits, in telling us something about the water pathway, but would not radioactive oxygen isotopes tell us still more?

There are no less than three radioactive oxygen isotopes known. All of them have eight protons in their nuclei, but some contain six neutrons, some seven and some eleven. The radioactive oxygen isotopes are oxygen-14, oxygen-15, and oxygen-19. Can they be used?

To answer that question, we must first understand that all radioactive atoms have a greater or lesser tendency to explode. Some actually have so small a tendency that they are almost stable; some have so large a tendency that it is impossible to collect more than a very few atoms at any one time.

Physicists measure the tendency to explode by calculating the time it would take for half the atoms in any particular quantity of a particular isotope to explode and change. This is the "half-life" of that isotope.

Uranium-238, the first substance to be discovered to be radioactive, has a half-life of 4,500,000,000 years. On the other hand, phosphorus-30, first formed by the Joliot-Curies, has a half-life of 2.55 minutes.

Half-lives must be taken into account in tracer experiments. If you try to use a radioisotope with a very long half-life, explosions are so few that they become difficult to follow. If you try to use one with a very short half-life, too many of the atoms are gone even before you can really get into the experiment. The most convenient half-lives range from a few days to a few thousand years. Then the isotope would hang around long enough to last through the experiment, and it would be breaking down quickly enough to follow with ease.

What, then, are the half-lives of the radioactive oxygen isotopes? The half-lives of oxygen-14, oxygen-15, and oxygen-19 are, respectively, 1.23 minutes, 2.05 minutes, and 0.50 minutes.

These half-lives are too short. The nature of the universe is simply against us here; and the radioactive oxygen isotopes cannot be used in the kind of experiments on photosynthetic water-splitting that can presently be conducted. What's more, physicists are quite certain that any additional radioactive oxygen isotopes that may be discovered in the future will have half-lives shorter still.

So it seems we are doomed—at least for now. Neither hydrogen nor oxygen offers us a chance to improve on the work done with oxygen-18. The intermediate details of water-splitting and oxygen-production in photosynthesis may continue to elude us for years.

Good Fortune with Carbon

But there is another part to the upward swing of the carbon cycle. The water molecule is split, yes, but then the hydrogen combines with carbon dioxide to form glucose. That second step introduces a third element—carbon. Can anything be done with carbon isotopes?

In 1929, the same year in which the stable oxygen isotopes were discovered, it was found that carbon was made up of two stable isotopes. The more common had nuclei containing six protons and six neutrons, so it was carbon-12. The less common (one atom out of every ninety) contained six protons and seven neutrons and was carbon-13.

Carbon-13 can be used as a tracer in the same way that oxygen-18 can. It has the usual inconveniences of a stable tracer, detection is slow and complicated.

There are, today, five known radioactive isotopes of carbon. These are carbon-10, carbon-11, carbon-14, carbon-15 and carbon-16. Of these, we can dismiss carbon-10, carbon-15, and carbon-16 out of hand. Their half-lives are impossibly short, being 19.1 seconds, 2.3 seconds and 0.7 seconds respectively.

That leaves carbon-11 and carbon-14 and of these two, only carbon-11 was known in the late 1930's It had a half-life of 20.5 minutes, which was still short, but it was the best available, and there was the temptation to try to use it.

Carbon, after all, is the key element of life. All organic compounds contain carbon atoms, and the chemical mechanisms within the tissues all involve the changes and viscissitudes of chains and rings of carbon atoms. It is more important for a biochemist to be able to follow the adventures and misadventures of the carbon atom than of all other atoms put together. This could be done with stable carbon-13, but only to a limited extent. Much more could be done with a radioactive isotope and so biochemists turned eagerly to carbon-11.

To use carbon-11, one would have to prepare it by bombarding the element, boron, with nuclei of hydrogen-2. The carbon-11 so formed is then combined with oxygen to form radioactive carbon dioxide.

As soon as carbon-11 atoms are formed, they begin to explode, of course, and each carbon-11 atom, as it explodes, is converted into stable boron-11. Suppose, then, that a certain quantity of carbon-11 has been formed. Twenty minutes after formation, half of the radioactivity is gone. In another twenty minutes, half of what is left is gone. After one hour, only $1/8$ of the original quantity is left and after two hours only $1/64$.

Consequently, there is need for great haste. Carbon-11 must be formed and converted into carbon dioxide; the radioactive carbon dioxide must be added to the system being experimented on; various chemical reactions must take place in tissue; the position and quantity of the carbon-11 atoms at the end of the experiment must be measured—and all in the space of two to two and a half hours at the most.

It is obvious that such experiments must be carried through with fiendish efficiency and that any misstep would be ruinous. It speaks well for the ingenuity of chemists and for their resistance to ulcers that experiments with carbon-11 were carried through and that some useful results were obtained.

Ruben and Kamen, for instance, (the two men who worked out the key oxygen-18 experiment on the production of oxygen in photosynthesis) also tried to work out the fate of the carbon dioxide by the use of carbon-11.

They found that carbon dioxide was fixed by green leaves not only in the light, but in the dark as well. They could tell this because they found carbon-11 in the leaf tissue components when they exposed the leaf to radioactive carbon dioxide in the dark. This made sense in view of the oxygen-18 experiments. Light was needed to split the water molecule and ATP was formed in the process. The ATP, once present, could power the addition of hydrogen to carbon dioxide to form glucose. Once sunlight had prepared a supply of ATP, the fixing of carbon dioxide would continue even in the absence of sunlight. Naturally, if the leaves were kept a sufficiently long period in the darkness, the reserve supplies of ATP would be consumed and carbon dioxide would no longer be fixed. If, after three hours of darkness, the leaves were exposed to carbon dioxide containing carbon-11, no carbon-11 would be found, later, among the tissue components.

But what compounds are formed on the way to glucose from carbon dioxide? By the 1930's, enough was known about the manner in which the chemical mechanisms of living tissue worked to make it quite clear that six carbon dioxide molecules were not going to form a glucose molecule by coming together in one grand crash. Rather, some simple molecule would first be formed and glucose would appear only after a number of steps.

Ruben and Kamen could tell that some simple compound was indeed formed, and could eliminate some possibilities as to the nature of that compound or compounds, but they were unable to make a positive identification.

The trouble was that when radioactive carbon dioxide was incorporated into molecules that made up part of the tissue substance, these molecules were intricately mixed with hundreds, or even thousands, of molecules that had not been formed from the radioactive carbon dioxide. It was necessary to take a small quantity of a very complex mixture and separate it into individual components, determining which contained carbon-11 and which did not, and then identifying those that did. This simply could not possibly be done in the amount of time granted by the short half-life of carbon-11.

What was really needed was a radioactive carbon isotope with a longer half-life than that of carbon-11, but there seemed no hope for the discovery of such an isotope. In the late 1930's, to be sure, carbon-14 had not yet been prepared. Physicists were quite certain that this isotope could be synthesized and would prove to be radioactive. Unfortunately, they were also quite certain that it would turn out to have a very short half-life. The atomic theories as then understood made this seem quite likely.

Nevertheless, in 1939, Kamen and Ruben began a systematic investigation of methods that might produce carbon-14. In 1940, they succeeded. They bombarded carbon with nuclei of hydrogen-2 and produced radioactive atoms which turned out to be carbon-14. To their delight and amazement, carbon-14 proved to be long-lived, much longer-lived than anyone would have predicted. The half-life is now known to be 5,770 years.

Chemists could scarcely believe their good fortune. This was short enough to produce sufficiently numerous explosions to follow easily. It was also long enough so that any reasonable experiment could be conducted with all desirable leisure. The existence of carbon-14 changed the face of biochemistry and it has proved to be by far the most useful and important radioactive isotope in existence.

As if that were not enough, another nearly incredible stroke of good fortune followed within four years.

Through the 1920's and 1930's biochemists used a technique called "chromatography" whereby a complex mixture of similar substances could be separated into individual components. Chromatography employed a column of some powdered substance such as aluminum oxide or starch. Down that column, a solution of the mixture was allowed to percolate and the various components of the mixture all clung to the surface of the powder particles with differing degrees of strength.

Additional samples of pure solvent (the substance in which the mixture had been dissolved) was then added to the column and allowed to trickle downward. There would be a certain tendency for each component of the mixture to be washed down by the trickling solvent. The extent to which each substance would be washed downward would depend on the relative tendency to cling to the powder and to dissolve in the solvent. These tendencies differed slightly for each component so that each was washed down at a slightly different rate. Gradually, as all moved downward, they separated, and, at the bottom of the tube, each component emerged alone.

It was a convenient technique and quite efficient, but it needed fairly sizable quantities of mixed substances and there was considerable tedium involved in the pouring of solvent and the catching of the final drippings in numerous small vessels, each of which had to be separately analyzed.

Two English biochemists, Archer John Porter Martin and Richard Laurence Millington Synge, were striving to find methods that would simplify chromatography and would work, with accuracy, on smaller quantities.

By 1944, they had perfected a method in which a large sheet of filter paper was used. A single drop of a complex mixture was placed in one corner of such a sheet and allowed to dry. The edge of the sheet was then placed in a trough of solvent and the whole placed in a closed container.

The solvent crept up the filter paper (which has a porous, blotting-paper texture), past the dried spot of mixed substances, and beyond.

There is a thin film of water (too thin to be noticeable) on the filter paper, and as the solvent passes the dried spot of the mixture, each component in the mixture has a certain tendency to dissolve in the solvent and move with it, and also a competing tendency to remain in the water film and stay where it is. The result of this irresolution, so to speak, is that each component moves with the solvent, but at a slower rate than the solvent itself moves, and some components, of course, move more slowly than others.

In the end, what began as a single spot of a complex mixture becomes a number of spots of individual substances. (Or, perhaps, a final spot may consist of a mixture of two or three substances that happened to move at equal speeds.)

The sheet of paper may then be dried, turned through ninety degrees, and a new edge placed in a second solvent, different from the first. Each of the many spots formed from the single original is now subjected to the action of this new moving solvent. If two or more substances had happened to move at equal speeds under the influence of the first solvent and ended up in the same place, they are exceedingly unlikely to move at the same speed in response to the second solvent also. This time they will separate.

By the end of the second stage, spots are distributed over the length and breadth of the paper and it is almost certain that each spot will represent a separate substance. The individual spots can be made visible by a variety of methods. They may be colored, to begin with. Or they may be made to react with some chemical so as to become colored. Or they may glow or seem black under ultraviolet light.

Once the spots are located, they can be cut out of the paper and the substance dissolved out of it in some suitable solvent. The substance can then be identified. Once the identity of the spots has been determined, a map can be prepared. When later separations are conducted and the location of the spot formed by each component is known, the composition of the mixture can be read off directly.

This process, known as "paper chromatography," will deal accurately with far smaller quantities of mixture than are required for ordinary "column chromatography." Paper chromatography, what is more, requires very little supervision and works automatically. It has become one of the most widely used and most nearly indispensable techniques in biochemistry and Martin and Synge were awarded the 1953 Nobel Prize in chemistry as a result.

What with paper chromatography and the use of isotopic tracers, biochemistry has advanced at an unbelievable pace since the mid-1940's. It is frightening to think how little of what we know today about life processes would have been learned without these two techniques.

It did not take long for chemists to realize that paper chromatography could be particularly useful for living tissue which had been exposed to a radioactive tracer. The substances which had incorporated the radioactive tracer would advertise themselves unmistakably, for they would be found in those spots where radioactivity could be detected. One could, in other words, go quickly over the final spot pattern and concentrate only on those spots which, by their radioactive nature, could be seen to include the tracer atoms in their substance.

It was with radioactive carbon-14 and paper chromatography, then, that the problem of carbon dioxide fixation in photosynthesis was now tackled.

The Carbon Dioxide Trap

The earliest attempts to make use of carbon-14 to unravel the photosynthetic jungle did not work out well. The mere fact that carbon-14 had so long a half-life encouraged the researchers to take their time and conduct prolonged experiments with cells photosynthesizing for hours. It was a relief, after all, to be done with the super-hasty experiments enforced by carbon-11's short half-life.

As it turned out, this was a mistake. Carbon dioxide containing carbon-14 entered plant tissue and in the course of hours engaged in a variety of interactions to form a complex mixture of substances. Each substance would then interact additionally, branching out further. Before long, carbon-14 could be found in almost every substance in the plant tissue and there was no way of telling into which it entered as a result of the direct photosynthetic pathway, and in which it entered through side-currents and bypaths.

The first to realize this clearly was a group of American biochemists at the University of California, under the leadership of Melvin Calvin and A. A. Benson. It occurred to them that what was needed was to expose the cells to radioactive carbon dioxide for just a few seconds of full photosynthesis and no more. Only the very first steps would have to be taken with the cells. (This did not mean a return to very haste-ridden experiments. The cells would be killed after a few seconds but then, thanks to carbon-14's long half-life, chemists could take all the time they needed to sort out the mixture within the cells.)

Calvin and Benson began such experiments in 1948, using algae for the purpose. Algae are one-celled plants that offer certain advantages in photosynthetic experiments. They are very active cells which live normally in water suspension; and water suspension offers an easy medium in which to work. Then, too, the algae cells are complete organisms in themselves, so there is no reason to think that their photosynthetic mechanism is not entirely intact. (Of course, it remains possible that photosynthesis is basically different in algae and in "higher plants." Enough work was done with whole leaves and mashed-up leaves to make this possibility seem very unlikely.)

Calvin's group started their algae working under good illumination and ordinary carbon dioxide till the cells were plugging away in fine fettle as was indicated by the production of oxygen at a steady and rapid rate. A stopcock was then opened and the suspension of algae was allowed to drain out through long tubes into a container of boiling methyl alcohol, which killed them at once.

Into the tubes through which the algae suspension was passing, radioactive carbon dioxide (which we can write as C^*O_2) was allowed to enter. The algae were thus exposed to C^*O_2 for only the few seconds it took to pass through the tubes and into the boiling alcohol.

Presumably, in the few seconds of exposure to carbon-14, there would only be time to participate in the very opening steps of the photosynthetic mechanism. There would be little or no side-mechanisms to confuse matters.

The dead algae cells are then filtered away from the alcohol and thoroughly mashed up in such a way as to break up all the cells and release the contents. The contents dissolved readily in appropriate solvents and another filtration removed the insoluble fragments of the cell structure. It is reasonable to suppose that the compounds being sought by the experimenters would be found in the solvent, for the first products of photosynthesis must surely be small and readily-soluble compounds. Indeed, this was not guess-work, for that much had been demonstrated by the early carbon-11 experiments.

A drop of the dissolved mixture of cell substances was placed on filter paper and dried. It was then subjected to paper chromatography in two dimensions so that a map of spots was formed. Since only the spots bearing radioactivity were of immediate interest, the dried filter paper with the spots was pressed down upon a sheet of photographic film. The radiations from the radioactive spots discolored the film, and a record was thus made of the radioactive spots only. The materials formed from the $C*O_2$ were made to take their own photograph, so to speak, and such a process is called "autoradiography."

After a five-second exposure of algae cells to $C*O_2$, it was discovered that some 90 per cent of the carbon-14 in the chromatographed material was concentrated in a single spot. The material in this spot was soaked out and analyzed and found to be phosphoglyceric acid (often abbreviated as "PGA") one of the compounds that is among the intermediates of anaerobic glyclosis. The formula of the compound is given in Figure 27.

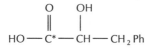

Figure 27. Phosphoglyceric Acid (PGA)

If you compare this formula with that in Figure 17 on page 92, you will see that there is a difference in the position of the phosphate group (Ph). In Figure 17, the Ph is on the second carbon from the left, while in Figure 27 it is on the third. The two molecules can therefore be distinguished as 2-phosphoglyceric acid and 3-phosphoglyceric acid respectively. For our purposes, though, we need not be so formal; PGA will be sufficient for both molecules.

By carefully breaking down the molecule of PGA into smaller

fragments, it was possible to determine which of the three carbon atoms in the molecule was carbon-14. This was found to be the carbon on the left and it is that one which is marked by an asterisk in the formula.

In photosynthesis, then, we begin with CO_2 and form PGA out of it. How is that done? One way of getting a hint of the process is to subtract CO_2 from the PGA and see what is left. The remainder is a compound called "glycol phosphate." We might, therefore, set up a hypothetical reaction in which carbon dioxide combines with glycol phosphate to form PGA, as in Figure 28. Glycol phosphate would, in this way, serve as a "carbon dioxide trap."

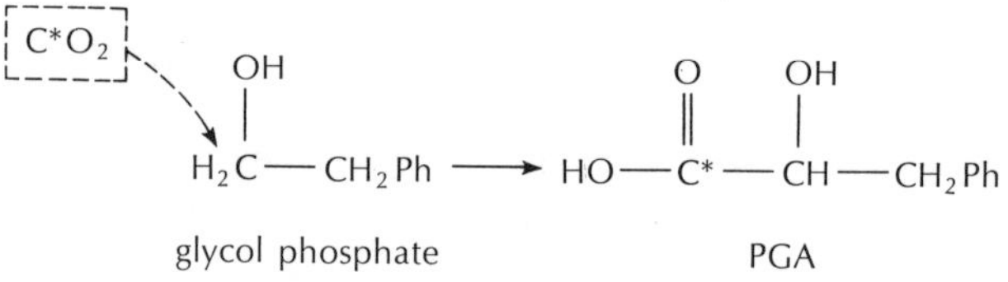

Figure 28. Glycol Phosphate

The only catch to this straightforward suggestion is that glycol phosphate cannot be located anywhere in plant tissue by even the most delicate chromatographic procedures.

The search was on, therefore, for other substances that played a part in the photosynthetic mechanism. One of these might be the carbon dioxide trap.

The candidates were numerous. If, instead of allowing photosynthesis to proceed for only a couple of seconds, it were allowed to go on for a minute and a half, at least fifteen different radioactive substances were located. Most of these proved to be well-known substances that, like PGA itself, were similar or identical to intermediates in the anaerobic glycolysis chain. Once PGA was formed, in other words, it was easy to see that it was converted to glucose by a reversal of well-known reactions.

It was the formation of PGA that remained the intermediate problem. In 1951, the University of California group finally identified a substance that was *not* clearly a member of the anaerobic glycolytic chain. This alone was sufficient to cause a firing-up of interest in it. On careful analysis, it turned out to be "ribulose-1, 5-diphosphate" or "RDP."

This was a substance in the glucose family (it was a "sugar") but it had one carbon atom fewer than glucose. Its molecule was made up of a chain of 5 carbons whereas the glucose molecule had 6. The molecule also had two phosphate groups attached. Its formula is shown in Figure 29.

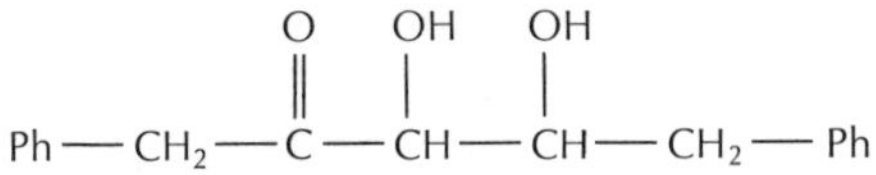

$$Ph - CH_2 - \overset{\displaystyle O}{\overset{\displaystyle \|}{C}} - \overset{\displaystyle OH}{\overset{\displaystyle |}{CH}} - \overset{\displaystyle OH}{\overset{\displaystyle |}{CH}} - CH_2 - Ph$$

Figure 29. Ribulose-1, 5-Diphosphate (RDP)

Let's think this through, now. The obvious possibility had, it seemed, put glycol phosphate in the position of being the carbon dioxide trap. Glycol phosphate has a 2-carbon chain and 1 phosphate group. Add carbon dioxide and you would have a 3-carbon chain and 1 phosphate group, and that fits well with PGA.

If, instead, RDP is the carbon dioxide trap, can that fit as well? Let's see. If you begin with RDP, you have a 5-carbon chain and 2 phosphate groups. Add carbon dioxide and you have a 6-carbon chain and 2 phosphate groups. But cut that molecule exactly in half and you have two molecules, each one of which possesses a 3-carbon chain and 1 phosphate group. In other words, for glycol phosphate the addition is $(2, 1)+(1, 0)=(3, 1)$; while for RDP, it is $(5, 2) + (1, 0) = (3, 1) + (3, 1)$.

Both systems work out neatly on paper, but there was one advantage of RDP over glycol phosphate as a possible carbon dioxide trap: RDP definitely exists in plant tissue.

To determine whether RDP was indeed the carbon dioxide trap, in the plant as well as on paper, biochemists had to determine the manner in which existing chemical mechanisms within the plant cell could add CO_2 to RDP. Then they had to follow the logical path from the 6-carbon molecule to the 3-carbon

PGA and see which carbon atom would end up radioactive. Was that radioactive carbon atom in the right place?

Everything checked out and chemists are now quite convinced that RDP is indeed the carbon dioxide trap.

The trap works as follows: Begin with RDP, with its carbon atoms numbered from 1 to 5, as in formula "a" in Figure 30. Next visualize a molecule of C^*O_2 (whose carbon atom we can number 6) adding itself to carbon-2 of RDP. Visualize also the two hydrogen atoms in association with carbon-3 moving over to carbon-2, as in formula "b" of Figure 30.

An "addition compound" is formed which is shown in formula "c" of Figure 30. This addition compound splits at the junction of carbon-2 and carbon-3, adding on a molecule of water as it does so. Of the water molecule (H_2O), a hydrogen atom (H) adds on at one side of the split and a hydroxyl group (OH) at the other, as in formula "d" of Figure 30. (The chemical mechanism that involves a molecular split with the addition of water is called "hydrolysis," from Greek words meaning "split by water.")

The resulting two molecules are shown in formula "e" of Figure 30. Both molecules in formula "e" are the same. One is written in such a way that the carbon chain bends and one is written from right to left while the other is from left to right, but they are the same compounds. Both are PGA. One possesses the radioactive carbon atom that originated in the C^*O_2 and it is in the position where it is supposed to be.

We can say, in short, that a molecule of RDP plus CO_2 plus H_2O gives us two molecules of PGA.

This leaves us with two problems:

1. In order to pass from carbon dioxide to glucose, four hydrogen atoms must be added for every carbon atom (see Equation 29 on page 139). So far, in forming the PGA, we've added CO_2 and H_2O to RDP, but we haven't added hydrogen atoms as such. (There are hydrogen atoms in the water molecule, but that is not the same thing. The water molecule, with its hydrogen atoms, is, in fact, given off again later.) Where, then, are hydrogen atoms added?

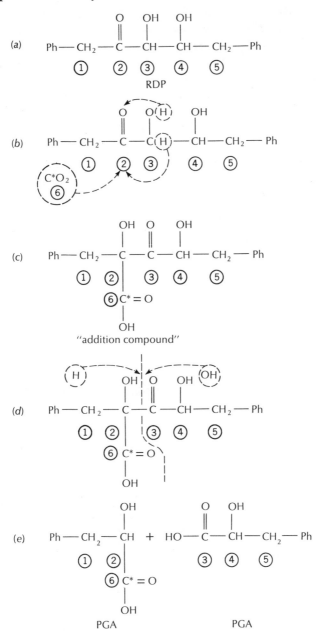

Figure 30. The Carbon Dioxide Trap

2. If RDP is the carbon dioxide trap, it must be available at all times to absorb the enormous quantities of carbon dioxide needed to form plant tissues. Yet RDP is present in very small concentrations in plant tissue. Clearly, it must be re-formed as quickly as it is used up.

It was the next task of the Calvin group to answer these questions. Continuing to identify the substances in the various spots after several minute-long exposures to C^*O_2, and pinpointing the exact positions of carbon-14 in the various molecules, they decided that once a molecule of PGA was formed, it added two hydrogen atoms to form a water molecule and one of a compound usually referred to as triose phosphate, or "TP." We can show this process in the simplest possible way (simpler, in fact, than the process which actually takes place) in Figure 31.

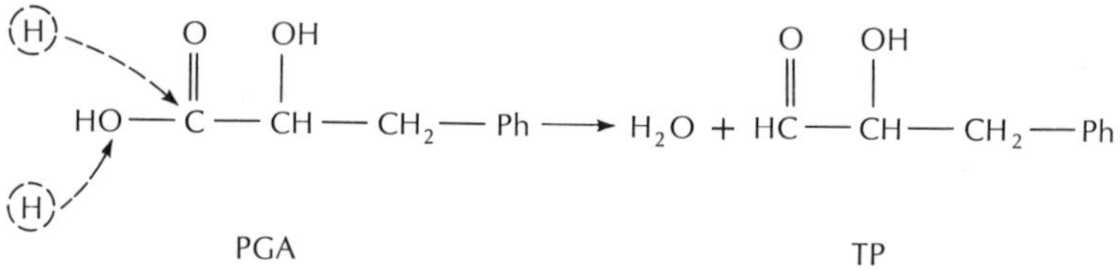

Figure 31. Triose Phosphate (TP)

As you see, it takes two hydrogen atoms to convert one molecule of PGA to TP plus H_2O. The addition of CO_2 to the carbon dioxide trap, RDP, produces *two* molecules of PGA, however. Together, naturally, they consume four hydrogen atoms. For each molecule of CO_2 absorbed, then, four hydrogen atoms must be used, and this is what is required to make the scheme worked out by Calvin and the rest correspond to reality.

This addition of hydrogen atoms requires an input of energy and that is supplied by ATP. (The actual energy relationships involved in the fixing of carbon dioxide are not yet worked out in satisfactory detail, but it is quite clear that the absorption of eight or nine quanta from sunlight will supply all the ATP needed for carbon dioxide fixation.)

Once TP is formed, two of these molecules can join together to form (after a series of changes) one molecule of RDP, consuming ATP here, too. The carbon dioxide trap is, thus, reopened. The RDP molecule that had been used to absorb a CO_2 molecule is re-formed and ready for another CO_2 molecule.

This is much more than merely going in a circle, though. The two TP molecules taken together have 6 carbons, the RDP only 5. What happens to the sixth carbon, which we may consider as having been the CO_2 molecule which was absorbed in the first place? It contributes to the formation of glucose. It becomes, in other words, a sixth-glucose.

We can put this another way by saying that if we start off with twelve molecules of TP (36 carbon atoms altogether), then these combine to form six molecules of RDP (30 carbon atoms altogether) plus one glucose molecule (6 carbon atoms). After all, $36 = 30 + 6$.

Notice also that the water molecule which was consumed in converting carbon dioxide plus RDP into two molecules of PGA is now given off again. (Or, more accurately, one is consumed and two given off, corresponding to a net production of one water molecule.)

We now have the key steps involved in the conversion of carbon dioxide to glucose. By showing only those key steps and leaving out a considerable number of intermediate steps that have been worked out in painstaking detail (and that won for Calvin the 1961 Nobel Prize in chemistry) we can present the simplified scheme of what is often called the "Calvin cycle" (see Figure 32).

For each turn of the Calvin cycle involving a single RDP molecule, one molecule of carbon dioxide and four hydrogen atoms are absorbed and one sixth-glucose and one water molecule are given off, which is precisely the situation given in Equation 29 on page 139.

Finally, then, we can combine the Calvin cycle with the carbon cycle to present in what will be, for this book, its final form

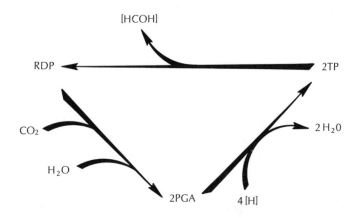

Figure 32. The Calvin Cycle

(see Figure 33). Much remains to be done, of course, and there are many details yet to be filled in, but we have now carried the description of the carbon cycle as far as we intended.

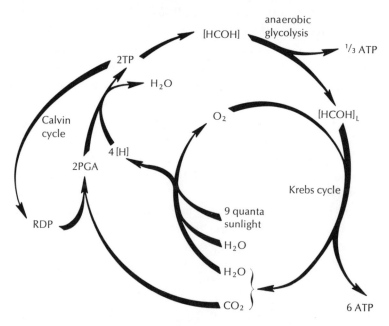

Figure 33. The Carbon Cycle (with the Calvin Cycle)

7

The Beginning of the Cycle

The Forming of the Earth

But how did it all begin?

The grand cycle that maintains life on Earth, that turns sunlight into chemical energy, that supplies us with an ever-full banquet-table and an ever-rich atmosphere—Can it just have *happened?*

Or must we suppose that only purpose and design can account for a mechanism so great and wonderful and so enormously complex?

It is important to decide between the alternatives if we can. If it is purpose, then it may be that only on this one planet in the entire Universe has such a design been carried out—Or maybe not. We would not be able to tell.

If, on the other hand, the cycle evolved through purely natural events and by random processes, we may be able to predict with some assurance whether it can take place on other planets too.

In our culture, it has been traditional to explain all beginnings as the result of design. A divine Creator is taken to be responsible for everything. To quote the Gospel of St. John 1:13:

All things were made by him; and without him was not anything made that was made.

This view has been held so deeply and intensely, and for such a long time, that there is still the flavor of sacrilege about question-

163

ing it. Nevertheless, scientists have, for the last two centuries, been attempting to work out from observation and experiment possible ways in which the solar system, including the Earth and everything on it, may have been formed through natural, undesigned, random events.

The scientist concerns himself with those aspects of the Universe that can be reduced to certain grand generalizations called "natural laws." It is quite safe to assume that we do not yet know all the natural laws, and that we do not perfectly understand the natural laws we know. Nevertheless, with what we have in hand, we fumble for greater knowledge.

We begin by assuming the existence of matter and energy in the Universe and suppose that they obey the various natural laws. What follows?

If we concentrate on the solar system, we suppose that to begin with there was a vast swirling cloud of dust and gas. This slowly contracted as a result of gravitational force into the Sun, while turbulent eddies on the outskirts of the cloud condensed into the various planets and satellites. In this fashion the solar system, including the Earth, was formed. Scientists have decided that this happened five or six billion years ago, basing their decision on the information gained from the amount of decay of certain radioactive substances which decay very slowly at accurately known rates.

This tells us something at once. It means that our planet and the life on it, as we know it today, have had some five or six billion years in which to develop.

That is important. Creation by design could conceivably take place in a short time (and our Bible tells us that heaven and earth were created in just six days). If, however, something as complex as the planet and the life on it were to reach their present form through the workings of blind chance, it is reasonable to expect that this would have to take a long time. Well, five or six billion years *is* a long time and we can be encouraged to continue the investigation of chance as the creator of life.

The next question to be asked concerns the chemical composition of the Earth as it formed, for it is out of the chemicals of the early Earth that life must have formed. We cannot rely entirely on the chemical composition of the Earth as it is today, for life did not form today. Life developed on a much younger Earth and it may well be that this much younger Earth was chemically different, perhaps radically so, from the planet we know.

No one was present at the forming of the Earth to make chemical tests, so we can progress only by making assumptions. One reasonable assumption is that the Earth was formed out of matter that very much resembled the matter in the Universe generally.

Astronomers have enough evidence to satisfy them that the Universe is made up almost entirely of hydrogen and helium, the two simplest kinds of atoms. This is true of the Sun, of many other stars that have been studied, of the gas between the stars, and so on. In fact, astronomers have even been able to estimate the relative numbers of all the various atoms.

If we imagine the matter of the Universe perfectly stirred up and take a sample that is large enough to contain 4,000,000 hydrogen atoms, the estimated number of atoms of other elements in the sample would be:

Helium	—	310,000
Oxygen	—	2,150
Neon	—	860
Nitrogen	—	660
Carbon	—	350
Silicon	—	100
Magnesium	—	91
Iron	—	60
Sulfur	—	37
Argon	—	15
Aluminum	—	10
Calcium	—	5
Sodium	—	4
Nickel	—	3
Phosphorus	—	1

If you were to begin with a larger sample of the Universe-material, you would include some of the still rarer elements. If you began with a quantity that contained 4,000,000,000,000 (four trillion) hydrogen atoms, you would find 1 uranium atom in the mass.

To be sure, this is the present makeup of the Universe rather than its past makeup. However, the Universe has lasted in essentially its present form for much longer than the solar system has. The Universe may be as much as twenty-five billion years old altogether, and a mere five or six billion years ago it wasn't very much different as far as average chemical composition is concerned. It was probably just a bit richer in hydrogen and a bit poorer in all the other elements.

We can assume, then, that the planets as they formed would be mostly hydrogen and helium, with a smattering of all the rest of the elements. And, as a matter of fact, the giant outer planets (Jupiter, Saturn, Uranus and Neptune) do indeed seem to have such a composition.

But Earth does not, and neither do the other relatively small inner planets (Mars, Venus and Mercury). In fact, hydrogen is comparatively rare on Earth and helium is almost non-existent. Why is this so?

For one thing, the inner planets are closer to the Sun and, therefore, may be expected to have been at a consistently higher temperature than the outer planets during the entire slow process of planetary formation. Hydrogen and helium, which are gases at all but extremely low temperatures, can only be held to a planet by gravitational forces, and the higher the temperature the faster the hydrogen molecules and helium atoms move and the more difficult they are to hold.

In the outer reaches of the solar system where the temperatures were low, hydrogen molecules and helium atoms were sluggish enough to be held. The planets built up to large masses because of the abundant hydrogen and helium which were there to be gathered up. This strengthened their gravitational field and made it all the easier for them to hold the gases. In the end giant planets were formed, planets overwhelmingly rich in hydrogen.

In the inner solar system where temperatures are comparatively high, hydrogen molecules and helium atoms were too nimble to be held and the planets formed of other elements. Because the elements other than hydrogen and helium make up only a small proportion of the matter of the original cloud out of which the Solar system formed, the inner planets ended up tiny for lack of raw material. They could build up only small gravitational fields, which did nothing to aid their cause in hydrogen and helium capture.

The inner planets were formed chiefly of those elements which could exist either by themselves or in combination with other elements as solids. The molecules and atoms of such solids cling together through electromagnetic forces that are trillions upon trillions of times stronger than gravitational forces.

For instance, silicon would combine with some of the oxygen (just some of it, for there isn't enough silicon to combine with all the oxygen) to form silicon dioxide. This would in turn combine with magnesium, iron, aluminum, calcium, sodium, nickel and many other of the rarer elements to form silicates. These silicates are rock-like in nature. Iron combines less readily to form silicates than do the other elements, but combine more readily with sulfur to form sulfides. A good deal of it is left over in the metallic form.

In the course of planetary formation metallic iron (mixed with its less common sister metal, nickel) would slowly settle to the center, for it is much denser than the silicates.

And so Earth today has a nickel-iron core, molten as a result of the high temperatures and pressures at the center. It makes up about 30 per cent of the mass of the entire planet. Next to it is the "mantle" which is made up of silicates; it surrounds the core very much as the white of the egg surrounds the yolk.

At the very surface of the Earth (corresponding to the shell of the egg) is a thin "crust" which makes up only 1/250 of the mass of the Earth and which is, on the average, only ten miles thick. The crust is also silicate in nature.

It may have taken a good long time for the Earth to conglomerate, for its parts to differentiate, and to take its present shape. It would be interesting to know just how long, for it is quite reasonable to suppose that life did not really get its start until the crust took its present form.

Rocks have been found in the crust today which are three and a half billion years old, judging by the radioactive matter they contain. That means that these rocks have been solid and in place for that length of time and the crust must be at least that old. A history of three and a half or, possibly, four billion years may still be long for life to form by random processes.

The Forming of the Atmosphere

But Earth is not entirely metal and rock. It contains a large quantity of liquid water and a deep gaseous atmosphere. How did they come to be?

As solid material conglomerated to form the Earth, it did so in a vast ocean of gas. The gathering Earth might not be able to hold those gases to itself by gravity, but the gases were there.

The gases consisted, first, of hydrogen in large preponderance. It also contained certain gases that do not, under ordinary circumstances, form compounds, but that remain gaseous and in elementary form at ordinary temperatures. These are, chiefly, helium, neon and argon.

Unlike helium and its sister elements, hydrogen can combine with other elements. Its vast preponderance makes such combination so highly probable that we can count on the presence of certain hydrogen-containing compounds among the gases. Naturally, those compounds will be most common which are made up of hydrogen and the most common of the remaining elements. If we eliminate helium and neon (which won't combine with hydrogen) the most common elements, after hydrogen, are oxygen, nitrogen, and carbon in that order.

Each of these can combine with hydrogen to form a compound that will be gaseous at ordinary temperatures. Oxygen combines with hydrogen to form water (H_2O) which is liquid at ordinary temperatures, but which always gives off quantities of water vapor which we can write as $H_2O[v]$. Nitrogen combines with hydrogen to form ammonia (NH_3), and carbon combines with it to form methane (CH_4). Both ammonia and methane remain gaseous at all ordinary Earth temperatures.

To begin with, Earth formed out of a gathering of particles of silicates and metal and had a gravitational field far too weak and diffuse to hold any of these gases as gases. However, water and ammonia, and, to a lesser extent, methane and hydrogen, could unite rather loosely with the silicates and other components of the forming Earth, so that at least *some* of their total mass would form part of the conglomerate. Helium, neon and argon formed no unions at all and were not included. (Small quantities of these gases are found in the atmosphere today, but they have been formed in recent times through radioactive decay of elements in the crust. They did not exist from the time of planetary formation.)

As the forming Earth grew larger and larger the conglomerating particles were more and more tightly compressed by the planet's intensifying gravitational field. The interior grew hotter and hotter so that the gases were squeezed and baked out.

After these gases emerged, there was still some question as to whether they might be held by the planet even after its gravitational field had attained its maximum intensity. Our Moon is so small, for instance, that the gases squeezed out of its conglomerating body could be held only briefly, and the Moon today has no atmosphere to speak of. (Astronomers suspect, though, that there may still be frozen water under the surface, or, at the very least, that considerable quantities of water may still be attached to the silicate molecules.)

Mercury is larger than the Moon, but being closer to the Sun, it is also hotter and it did not retain an appreciable atmosphere either. Mars is still larger and, being farther from the Sun, is cooler. It retained a thin atmosphere. Venus and Earth, being the largest of the inner planets and having the most intense gravitational fields, each kept a moderately thick atmosphere which was, however, much thinner than the enormous atmospheres of the outer planets.

Earth could not long keep the hydrogen that may have fizzed out of its compacting interior, but it could keep the other gases.

Assuming that the surface temperature was below 100° C. most of the water would be in liquid form and collect as an ocean. Considerable quantities of ammonia would dissolve in it, and lesser quantities of methane and (for a while) hydrogen would do so too. However, quantities of water vapor would remain in the atmosphere, and so would much ammonia and almost all the methane.

The original atmosphere of the primordial Earth would be made up mainly of $H_2O[v]$, NH_3 and CH_4. We can call this "Atmosphere I." This resembles the atmospheres of the outer planets, if we disregard the fact that the outer planets also have large amounts of hydrogen and helium in their atmospheres.

Yet this Atmosphere I which we have arrived at by deduction is not at all like Earth's atmosphere today. Is that deduction wrong, or has something happened to change the atmosphere? And, if something has happened to change it, why didn't that same thing also change Jupiter's atmosphere, for instance?

One thing that we have in much greater abundance than Jupiter is sunlight. What would be the effect of sunlight on Atmosphere I? In particular, what would be the effect of the energetic ultraviolet radiation of sunlight?

Ultraviolet radiation, penetrating the atmosphere, would strike a water molecule. The water molecule would absorb the ultraviolet and gain energy. The molecule would vibrate more energetically, as a result, and its atoms would shake themselves loose. In short, a water molecule under the influence of ultraviolet light would decompose into hydrogen and oxygen. This process is called "photodissociation."

When water breaks up into hydrogen and oxygen, the hydrogen cannot be held by Earth's gravitational field and escapes into space. The oxygen is held and it combines with other components of the atmosphere. It combines with methane to form carbon dioxide (CO_2) and water. It combines with ammonia to form nitrogen (N_2) and water. The actual course of events could be very complicated indeed, but in the end, all the ammonia and methane are consumed and in its place are nitrogen and carbon dioxide. A new atmosphere ("Atmosphere II") has been formed, which is $H_2O[v]$, N_2 and CO_2 (see Figure 34).

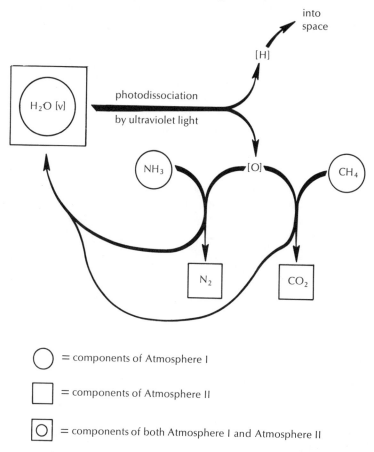

Figure 34. Atmosphere I to Atmosphere II

In the process of converting Atmosphere I into Atmosphere II, a great deal of water must be photodissociated. Some scientists have estimated that about half of Earth's original supply of water was used up in the conversion. Fortunately, enough remains to make up our still-mighty oceans.

The change from Atmosphere I to Atmosphere II has taken place on Mars and Venus, where the atmosphere is almost entirely carbon dioxide, plus a little nitrogen.

In outer planets the process must be much slower, since far less ultraviolet reaches those planets and the atmospheres are much larger to begin with. No perceptible change has taken place after billions of years and the outer-planet atmospheres are still Atmosphere I.

But Earth's present atmosphere is not Atmosphere II, either. Our present atmosphere ("Atmosphere III") contains oxygen in place of carbon dioxide. It is $H_2O[v]$, N_2 and O_2.

How was Atmosphere III formed? Is it possible that Atmosphere III formed naturally through photodissociation? After the changeover to Atmosphere II was complete would not water molecules continue to dissociate? Would not hydrogen continue to escape into space and oxygen continue to remain behind? If so, oxygen would no longer have anything in the atmosphere to combine with. Neither nitrogen nor carbon dioxide will combine with oxygen under ordinary circumstances. Oxygen would therefore merely accumulate in its free, molecular form, and the water supply of the Earth would continue to deplete.

We can see at once, though, that there is something wrong with this notion. Yes, oxygen might form; but what would have brought about the disappearance of carbon dioxide? In Atmosphere II carbon dioxide would have had to be present in great quantity. (On Venus and Mars it makes up the lion's share of the atmosphere.) In our present Atmosphere III, it makes up only 0.03 per cent of the whole. Any theory that would account for the conversion of Atmosphere II into Atmosphere III must account not only for the appearance of oxygen but for the disappearance of carbon dioxide.

What's more, the whole notion of the continued photodissociation of water must be abandoned as a possible cause of the change. As soon as oxygen begins to accumulate in free form through photodissociation of water some of it is converted into "ozone," a high-energy form of oxygen, with molecules made up of three oxygen atoms apiece, O_3.

Ozone strongly absorbs ultraviolet radiation so that, once it is formed, the atmosphere is cut off from that radiation. Photodissociation which depends on ultraviolet light must therefore stop.

That is, indeed, the situation now. There is an ozone layer about fifteen miles above the surface of the Earth. Air is thin up there and the ozone is present only in small quantities, but it is enough to absorb ultraviolet radiation. Very little of this ultraviolet radiation can penetrate into the lower atmosphere where water vapor is to be found.

Photodissociation is therefore a "self-limiting process." It works as long as the oxygen is consumed as quickly as it is formed. This is so as long as there is a steady changeover from Atmosphere I to Atmosphere II. Once Atmosphere II is completely formed, however, oxygen accumulates, ozone forms, and photodissociation stops.

But what, besides photodissociation, can form oxygen? To anyone who has been reading this book, the obvious answer is photosynthesis.

Photosynthesis forms oxygen out of water through the energy of visible light which is *not* absorbed by the ozone layer in the upper atmosphere and which continues to reach the Earth's surface. Photosynthesis is not self-limiting in the same way photodissociation is.

Then, too, photosynthesis does not liberate hydrogen as such but incorporates it into plant tissue from which it is eventually re-converted into water. Unlike photodissociation, photosynthesis does not deplete Earth's water supply.

Finally, photosynthesis not only liberates oxygen but also incorporates carbon dioxide into plant tissue. As a result, not only is oxygen produced but carbon dioxide is consumed.

In fact, photosynthesis accounts so neatly for the conversion of Atmosphere II into Atmosphere III (see Figure 35) that it scarcely seems reasonable to search for any alternative explanation. Scientists are quite satisfied that Earth's atmosphere has achieved its present composition through the agency of life.

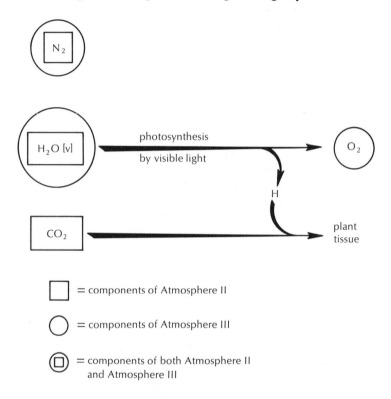

Figure 35. Atmosphere II to Atmosphere III

But that means life must have existed before our present Atmosphere III did! Life must have formed during the existence of Atmosphere I, or Atmosphere II, or perhaps during the period of transition from one to the other.

And how might that have happened?

The Forming of Life

The first to suggest seriously that life might have had its start in an atmosphere other than the present one was the English biochemist John B. S. Haldane. In the 1920's he pointed out that if life was responsible for the oxygen in the atmosphere, it ought to have started when there was no oxygen in it and when carbon dioxide was present instead. In other words, he suggested that life started in Atmosphere II.

In 1936 a Russian biochemist, Alexander Ivanovich Oparin, published a book called *The Origin of Life*. In it he reasoned that Earth's original atmosphere contained methane and ammonia and suggested that it was in this Atmosphere I that life had made its beginning.

In either case, the molecules that served as raw material were small ones: water, nitrogen, and carbon dioxide in Atmosphere II, and water, ammonia, and methane in Atmosphere I. Yet the end result, if life were to be produced, must be enormous molecules of such substances as protein and nucleic acid.

Put in its simplest form, then, the creation of life involved the formation of large molecules out of small ones, and this requires an input of energy.

There are at least four important sources of energy on the primordial Earth: 1) the internal heat of the Earth, 2) the electrical energy of thunderstorms, 3) the radioactive breakdown of certain isotopes in the Earth's crust, and 4) the ultraviolet radiation from the Sun. All four sources were probably present in greater quantity in the distant past than today.

The first who actually tried to imitate primordial conditions in a laboratory experiment was Calvin, the same man who did such important work in connection with the carbon dioxide trap (see page 153). He chose as his raw materials a portion of Atmosphere II: carbon dioxide and water vapor. As his energy source

Calvin decided to use the fast-flying particles emitted by radioactive isotopes.

Calvin exposed his mixture of water and carbon dioxide to radiation from radioactive isotopes and, after a while, tested the mixture to see if anything new had formed. He found that some simple organic molecules had appeared, molecules somewhat larger and more complex than the original ones. He found, for instance, molecules of formaldehyde (HCHO) and of formic acid (HCOOH).

This was a promising beginning. Simple molecules could be made more complicated by energy input of a type available on the primordial Earth.

But did this imply that Atmosphere II was the environment in which life was created? Not necessarily. Calvin did not include the nitrogen of that atmosphere as one of his raw materials. Perhaps nothing much would have happened if he had for molecular nitrogen is rather inert and forms compounds only reluctantly. Yet nitrogen is a necessary component of proteins and nucleic acids, and if it is not included in available form in the raw material, life as we know it could not have formed.

The nitrogen-containing component of Atmosphere I, ammonia, will react readily with other molecules. It is a much more practical nitrogenous raw material than molecular nitrogen would be. On the other hand, the carbon-containing component of Atmosphere I, methane, is somewhat less active than the carbon dioxide of Atmosphere II. So far, it is something of a standoff.

But let's consider the different energy sources. Radioactive energy would be most readily available where radioactive minerals were most concentrated and this would be in only a few comparatively small portions of the Earth's surface. Similarly, the Earth's internal heat might be most readily available near volcanic regions, and yet not *too* near them. Again the ideal conditions would be confined to only a small portion of the planetary surface. Thunderstorms might strike almost anywhere, but in any given place the energy of the lightning bolt would appear only briefly and intermittently. All three of these sources of energy are limited, therefore, either in space or in time.

In contrast, however, ultraviolet light from the Sun bathed all the Earth, and did so for twelve hours at a time in any given spot, on the average. Ultraviolet energy is widespread, both in space and time.

It would seem then that ultraviolet light is the most likely energy source for the manufacture of large molecules in quantity. But if this is so then we must eliminate Atmosphere II as the raw material. In a fully formed Atmosphere II an ozone layer forms in the upper atmosphere, and this blocks the ultraviolet light and prevents it from reaching the lower atmosphere and the ocean where the essential water molecules are.

This means that life must have been formed while Atmosphere I was in existence and was in the process of changeover into Atmosphere II. In turn, this means that methane and ammonia must be included among the raw materials, and that they might, along with water, of course, even be the chief raw materials.

In 1953 Urey (who two decades before had first detected deuterium, see page 144) felt the need of trying out this notion in the laboratory. He suggested to one of his students, Stanley Lloyd Miller, that an experiment be set up in which energy was added to a sample of Atmosphere I.

Miller placed a mixture of ammonia, methane, and hydrogen in a large glass vessel. In another, he boiled water. The steam that formed passed up a tube connecting the two vessels and into the gas mixture. The gas mixture was pushed by the steam through another tube back into the boiling water. The second tube passed through a surrounding bath of cold water so that the steam condensed into liquid before dripping back into the boiling water. The gas mixture bubbled through the boiling water and around the course again, driven always by freshly formed steam.

Naturally, Miller made very certain that everything he used was completely sterile; that there were no living cells in the system to form complicated compounds. If complicated compounds formed, it would have to be in the utter absence of life.

It would have been reasonable to use ultraviolet light as the energy source, but ultraviolet light is easily absorbed by glass and this raised the problem of getting enough energy through the glass and into the gas mixture. Miller therefore decided to try the use of an electric spark that would serve as an imitation of the kind of energy made available by lightning. Through the gas in one portion of the system, he set up a continuing electric spark.

Things began to happen at once. The water and gases were colorless to begin with, but by the end of one day the water had turned pink. As the days continued to pass, the color grew darker till it was a deep red.

After a week Miller was ready to subject his mixture to analysis by paper chromatography (see page 151). Like Calvin, he found simple organic molecules in his mixture. One of these was the formic acid which Calvin had detected. Other compounds, related to formic acid, but still more complicated, were also present. These included acetic acid (CH_3COOH), glycolic acid ($HOCH_2COOH$), and lactic acid ($CH_3CHOHCOOH$) all of which were substances that are intimately associated with life.

The presence of ammonia in the starting mixture meant that nitrogen atoms were also available for the build-up of more complex molecules, and Miller found nitrogen-containing compounds too in his final mixture. There were present hydrogen cyanide (HCN), for instance, and urea (NH_2CONH_2).

Most important of all, though, Miller discovered among his products two different amino acids. (Amino acids are the relatively small building blocks out of which the giant protein molecules are built up.) There are nineteen different amino acids that commonly appear, in varying numbers, in protein molecules and the two detected happened to be the two simplest: glycine and alanine.

Miller's experiment was significant in several ways. In the first place, these compounds had formed quickly and in surprisingly large quantity. One-sixth of the methane with which he had started had gone into the formation of more complex organic compounds, yet the experiment had only been in operation for a week.

How must it have been, then, on the primordial Earth, with its vast warm ammoniated ocean stirred by winds of methane, all baking under the Sun's ultraviolet radiation for many millions of years? Uncounted tons of complex compounds would surely have been formed and the oceans must have become a kind of "warm soup" of them.

Then, too, the kind of organic molecules formed in Miller's experiments were just those present in living tissue. The path taken by the simple molecules, as they grew more complex, seemed pointed dierctly toward life. This pointing-toward-life continued consistently in later, more elaborate experiments. At no time were molecules formed in significant quantity that seemed to point in an unfamiliar, non-life direction.

Thus, Philip Hauge Abelson, working at the Carnegie Institution of Washington, followed Miller's work by trying a variety of similar experiments with starting materials made up of different gases in different combinations. It turned out that as long as he began with molecules that included atoms of carbon, hydrogen, oxygen and nitrogen, amino acids of the kind found normally in proteins were formed.

Nor were electric discharges the only source of energy that would work. In 1959, two German scientists, W. Groth and H. von Weyssenhoff, designed an experiment in which ultraviolet light could be used after all, and they got amino acids also.

It is important to progress farther and go beyond the very simplest products. One way of doing so would be to start with larger samples of raw materials and subject them to energy for longer periods. This would produce increasing numbers of more and more complicated products; but the mixtures of these products would become increasingly complex and would be increasingly difficult to analyze.

Instead, chemists began with later stages. The products formed in earlier experiments would be used as new raw materials. Thus, one of Miller's products was hydrogen cyanide. At the University of Houston, the Spanish-born biochemist J. Oro added hydrogen cyanide to the starting mixture in 1961. He obtained a richer mixture of amino acids and even a few compounds consisting of individual amino acids hooked together in short chains in just the same way in which they are hooked together within the protein molecules.

He also formed purines, compounds containing a double-ring

system of carbon and nitrogen atoms, and which are found within the various nucleic acid molecules. A particular purine called "adenine" was obtained, one that is found not only in nucleic acids but in other important compounds associated with life.

In 1962, Oro used formaldehyde as one of his raw materials and produced two five-carbon sugars, ribose and deoxyribose, both of which are essential components of nucleic acids.

In 1963, the Ceylon-born biochemist Cyril Ponnamperuma, at Ames Research Center in California, working with Ruth Mariner and Carl Sagan, began with adenine and ribose as his raw materials and exposed them to ultraviolet light. They linked up to form "adenosine" in the same fashion in which they are hooked together in nucleic acid molecules.

If phosphates were also included with the starting mixture, they too were added on to the adenosine to form "adenylic acid," one of the "nucleotides" that form the building blocks of nucleic acids. Indeed, by 1965, Ponnamperuma was able to announce that he had formed a double nucleotide, a structure in which two nucleotides are combined in exactly the same manner in which they are combined in nucleic acid molecules.

It was also possible to attach three phosphate groups to the adenosine to form nothing other than our old friend ATP out of a primordial mixture in the absence of life.

In short, the raw materials of Atmosphere I, exposed to almost any reasonable energy source (particularly to ultraviolet light) built up rapidly into more and more complicated molecules aimed directly at proteins and nucleic acids.

Experimenters in the laboratory have not yet formed natural proteins and nucleic acids in the complete absence of life, but the direction is unmistakable. Eventually, molecules sufficiently complicated to show the properties of life would be formed on the primordial Earth.

Thus, nucleic acids would surely develop finally, possessing molecules sufficiently complex to be capable of bringing about the production of other molecules exactly like themselves out of the raw materials all about. Such nucleic acid molecules maintain and multiply themselves and this is the minimum one could expect of a living thing. They would represent the first and simplest manifestation that we could call life.

When can all this have happened? Calvin has isolated complex hydrocarbons (molecules made up of carbon and hydrogen atoms only) imprisoned in rocks that are up to three billion years old. These are probably the remnants of very simple living things, living when the rock was first formed.

Considering that the Earth's crust may not be much over three and a half billion years old, this means that the "chemical evolution" which preceded the actual formation of life may have run its course in as little as half a billion years. This is not too surprising, when we think that small-scale chemical experiments have produced so much in experiments that lasted merely days and weeks.

In fact, "blind" chemical processes are not so blind. Given certain raw materials and a supply of energy, the changes that take place are just those that are most probable in the light of known chemical and physical laws, and these changes prove to be inevitably in the direction of life. Life is therefore the result of high-probability changes that are next to impossible to avoid if the conditions are right. By this view, life is no "miracle" at all.

The Forming of Cells

We have no way of telling what the compound was that first possessed the capability of producing others like itself. Today, the known compounds that do so belong to the class of nucleic acids. It seems reasonable to suppose that the first replicating molecule was a simple nucleic acid.

There is an exception, however, an unusually small virus-like particle that causes "scrapie," a disease of sheep. The particle replicates, for it can spread from sheep to sheep, with uncounted millions forming from a single particle. Yet, no nucleic acid has been located in scrapie virus.

Can it be, then, that in the early days of life-formation more than one type of molecule was developed with the capacity of replication? Perhaps replicating protein molecules were formed; or complex replicating sugar molecules. There may have been a race, of sorts, in which various kinds of replicating molecules made use of the raw materials available in the ocean. Those that were more efficient and speedier than the others would get the lion's share and would, in time, crowd out the rest.

It is easy to suppose that nucleic acid molecules, being the most efficient replicators, won out; but is efficiency of replication the only factor involved?

The naked replicating molecule labors under certain disadvantages. The building blocks it must use, and the high-energy molecules it must break down for the necessary energy supply, were all dispersed throughout the ocean and had to be gathered one at a time. Replication under these circumstances would be slow indeed, even at best.

But what if a supply of building blocks, of high-energy compounds, of all sorts of other useful substances, were gathered together in one reservoir and held together by some sort of membrane that walled it off from the ocean generally. Very inefficiently replicating molecules might then compete on an even basis with efficient replicators that had to forage over the ocean generally, so to speak.

Reservoirs of life-active materials, walled off by a membrane, are "cells." How might such cells have been formed?

Haldane, who started the modern attack on the problem of the origin of life, considered the question of cell-formation. He pointed out that when oil is added to water, thin films of oil sometimes form bubbles in which tiny droplets of water are enclosed.

A cell is, in a way, a bubble of water, with proteins and other materials in solution or suspension, surrounded by a complex film which is partly oily in character. Could today's complex cell be the result of billions of years of evolution that began with a "soap-bubble" in the ocean?

Sidney W. Fox of the University of Miami investigated the

origin of cells experimentally. It seemed to him that the early earth must have been quite hot and that the energy of heat alone could be sufficient to form complex compounds out of simple ones.

To test this, Fox, in 1958, heated a mixture of amino acids and found they formed long chains that resembled those in protein molecules. Fox called them "proteinoids" (meaning "protein-like") and found the likeness a very good one indeed. Stomach juices, which digest ordinary protein, would also digest protein-oids. Bacteria, which would feed and grow on ordinary protein, would also feed and grow on proteinoids.

Most startling of all, when Fox dissolved the proteinoids in hot water and let the solution cool, he found they would cling to-gether in little spheres about the size of small bacteria. Fox called these "microspheres."

These microspheres are not alive by the usual standards, but they behave as cells do, in some respects at least. They are sur-rounded by a kind of membrane, for instance. By adding certain chemicals to the solution, Fox could make the microspheres swell or shrink, much as ordinary cells do. They can produce buds, which seem to grow larger sometimes, and then break off. Micro-spheres can separate, divide in two, or cling together in chains.

Perhaps, then, the developments of life followed two pathways: one leading to the formation of nucleic acids, which are capable of efficient replication, and the other leading to the development of protein cells, which are inefficient in replication but store large supplies of all that is needed.

Could it be that a crucial day arrived when the two pathways accidentally coalesced into one? Cells of even the earliest type might well have been capable of ingesting smaller molecules they happened to bump into. It would be the most primitive form of "eating." The ingested molecules might be capable of yielding energy on breakdown, or of being incorporated in the cell's struc-ture. If not suitable for either purpose, it might eventually have been excreted.

Suppose that some protein cells "ate" nucleic acids, and that, after uncounted millions of such events, an eaten nucleic acid molecule happened to fit the cell structure so well as to remain a permanent part of it.

Such a "nucleic acid cell" would combine the superior replicative ability of nucleic acid with the vital supplies of the cell. The combination would be far more efficient than either the free nucleic acid molecule or the bare cell.

From this nucleic acid cell which, conceivably, may have formed just once, all the cells that exist today are descended. Perhaps, too, at some stage in the development, certain cells learned to grow as parasites within other cells, and, in doing so, gradually lost the material needed for independent life. The viruses of today may represent "stripped-down" descendants of that original nucleic acid cell. Almost back to the beginning, they consist of little more than nucleic acid itself. Sometimes a protein coat and an enzyme molecule or two are all that remains to indicate that the virus could once have been a cell.

The first cells may well have developed on an earth surrounded by Atmosphere I slowly changing into Atmosphere II. Under this condition, there would be no free oxygen available and energy would be derived from reactions that did not require that element—from reactions like anaerobic glycolysis, for instance.

The complicated compounds, broken down for energy, would be built up again by the action of ultraviolet light. Life could not, then, multiply beyond the level where it could be supplied by ultraviolet energy.

Once Atmosphere II was fully formed, life might have been in danger of extinction. With Atmosphere II established, the ozone umbrella would begin to form (see page 173) and the supply of ultraviolet light at the surface of the ocean would begin to fail. A planetary "famine" would come into being, a famine that would steadily intensify.

There was an alternative. Porphyrin compounds (see page 47) are stable and would form from simpler substances in the primordial ocean. In 1966, G. W. Hodson and B. L. Baker, in Edmonton, Alberta, began with pyrrole and paraformaldehyde (both of which can be formed from still simpler substances) and demonstrated the formation of porphyrin rings after merely gentle heating for three hours. If it was done in the presence of certain metal-containing compounds, the porphyrin rings would end up containing metallic atoms in the center.

Certain magnesium-porphyrins would form with the capacity for making use of the energy of visible light for the building up of complex compounds from simple ones—a primitive form of photosynthesis. These magnesium-porphyrins, constantly being ingested by cells, must, on at least one occasion, have remained to be incorporated into the cellular structure.

Even the inefficient use of visible light in the first magnesium-porphyrin cells must have given them a tremendous advantage over ordinary cells at a time when the ultraviolet light was slowly being shut off.

In the end, all our photosynthesizing cells may have originated from a single original, which may have been analogous to what we call, today, a chloroplast.

Signs of that original chloroplast remain. There are two thousand species of a group of one-celled photosynthesizing organisms called "blue-green algae." (They are not all blue-green, but the first ones studied were.) These are very simple cells, rather bacteria-like in structure, except that they contain chlorophyll and bacteria do not. Blue-green algae might almost be viewed as single, rather large, chloroplasts, and they may be the simplest descendants of the original chloroplast.

Still other descendants may have lost the chlorophyll and taken to parasitism or to foraging on dead tissue and its components. These would be the present-day bacteria.

As chloroplasts multiplied in the ancient seas, molecular oxygen produced by them must have begun to build up. Certain iron-porphyrins were capable of bringing about reactions, using molecular oxygen, that liberated more energy than anaerobic glycolysis did. These, eaten by cells, must on at least one occasion have converted an ordinary cell into an oxygen user.

We might call such an oxygen-using cell the first mitochondrion.

The chloroplasts and mitochondria which are today found within cells may themselves be the remnants of early cells, smaller and more primitive than any found today. Both chloroplasts and mitochondria contain nucleic acid of their own (of a type resembling the varieties found in bacteria) and they can apparently reproduce by mechanisms separate from the general reproductive scheme of the cell itself.

It may be, then, that along with the simple chloroplasts and

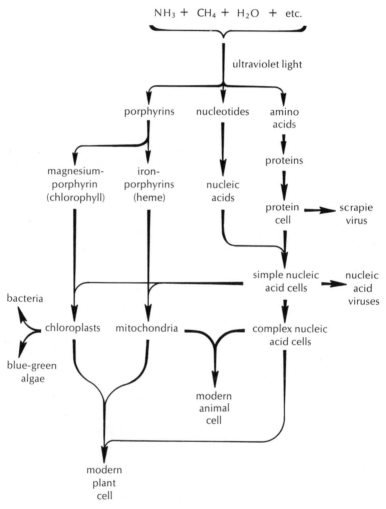

Figure 36. The Origin of Life

mitochondria formed in the slowly oxygenating seas, there would be certain large anaerobic cells, too. If the latter ingested the former and retained them, we would have the "modern cell" of today.

A schematic representation of the formation of life as pictured in this chapter is shown in Figure 36.

And if such a scheme is valid, depending as it does on random processes, why could it not happen on planets other than the Earth? It would seem that on any planet that is sufficiently Earth-like in properties and in chemistry, life would be bound to form. According to some estimates (those of Stephen H. Dole of Rand Institute, for instance) there may be as many as 640,000,000 Earth-like planets in our own Galaxy alone.

What precise form such life might take we cannot say, but the thought that it may exist there at all is an exciting one. The difficulties of exploration beyond the solar system are enormous, but the rewards in terms of knowledge are enormous, too.

Perhaps some day—some far-distant day—men will get out there to see.

Index